the
half
known
life

BY THE SAME AUTHOR

PICO
IYER

the
half
known
life

in search
of paradise

BLOOMSBURY CIRCUS
LONDON · OXFORD · NEW YORK · NEW DELHI · SYDNEY

BLOOMSBURY CIRCUS
Bloomsbury Publishing Plc
50 Bedford Square, London, WC1B 3DP, UK
29 Earlsfort Terrace, Dublin 2, Ireland

BLOOMSBURY, BLOOMSBURY CIRCUS and the Bloomsbury Circus
logo are trademarks of Bloomsbury Publishing Plc

First published in 2023 in the US as *The Half-Known Life* by
Riverhead Books, an imprint of Penguin Random House LLC
First published in Great Britain 2023
This edition published 2023

A catalogue record for this book is available from the British Library

ISBN: HB: 978-1-5266-5501-1; eBook: 978-1-5266-5499-1;
ePDF: 978-1-5266-5499-1

2 4 6 8 10 9 7 5 3 1

Typeset by Integra Software Services Pvt. Ltd.
Printed and bound in Great Britain by CPI Group (UK) Ltd, Croydon
CR0 4YY

To find out more about our authors and books visit www.bloomsbury.com
and sign up for our newsletters

for

NANDINI IYER,

fellow traveler

1931–2021

With all your science can you tell how it is—
& whence it is, that light comes into the soul?

—Henry David Thoreau, July 1851

contents

I

The Walled Garden

Four hours in Iran, and already I was having to rethink almost everything. The local guide who'd greeted me as I stumbled out of Customs at three in the morning, elegant in black slacks and jacket, had begun to speak about his days at a boarding school near London in the 1970s. We'd pulled up at a luxury hotel, and I'd heard the strains of "Yesterday" being plaintively piped through the lobby. In one corner of the palatial space, a small sign in English pointed to a tiny room: "Mosque." Very close to it, a Swarovski shop was dripping in crystals and an Yves Rocher boutique promised this season's offerings from Paris.

Now, as I strolled back from an early morning walk in the late summer sunlight, past a series of blue-glass towers lining the spotless, near-empty street, I saw Ali, my official Virgil, striding towards me with a smile. The lobby behind him was full, when we re-entered, of women tapping away

3

on smartphones with rose-colored fingernails, strands of silky hair slipping out from under many a hijab.

"Shall we make our first stop this morning"—Ali's English would not have sounded out of place in Windsor Castle—"Tus?"

"Actually, I was hoping we could go to the Imam Reza Shrine." Over eighteen months of correspondence with the Foreign Ministry in Tehran, I'd taken pains to ensure my trip would begin in the holy city. I was less interested in a shadowy government that seemed to shift policies with every passing season than in a culture that had dazzled me from afar since boyhood with its jeweled verses and the flat visions of paradise magicked into being on its carpets. The central mosque in Mashhad, with its fourteen minarets, four seminaries, seven interlocking marble courtyards and cemetery, was said to be the largest such compound on the planet.

"There are," said Ali, with what sounded like sculpted vagueness, "a few complications today. Perhaps we should drive out into the country?"

Captive for now, I followed my companion out to a car, where a burly older man, sporting a baseball cap—"Australia"—above his white shirt and chinos, was waiting to guide us through wide, tree-lined streets under large freeway signs in English. We passed a commanding statue, and Ali reminded me that Omar Khayyam, cradling an astronomical instrument above the modern boulevard, had invented a calendar more accurate than the Gregorian. Khayyam might be famous in England for his romantic quatrains—"Take care to create your own paradise, here and now on earth"—but in Iran he was best known for his transformative calculations.

We continued along quiet country roads that my guide could have likened to Oxfordshire, though these ones were lined with orchards of peaches and cherries. Ali spun beautifully brocaded sentences about double meanings and starlit nights, about how the same Farsi word was used for both "garden" and "paradise." All Iran was a garden in the poetry of its local hero Ferdowsi, he explained; the same man had laid down both the outlines of a legal system and a code of courtly love. No, of course, our hotel wasn't quite the London Hilton on Park Lane—he stayed there often while taking Iranians on tours of Britain—but he hoped it might prove comfortable enough.

We were traveling out to the small town of Tus, Ali went on, because it was there that Ferdowsi was buried. Jalaludin Rumi might be famous across the West; his verses about giving himself up to the "Beloved" and flinging away holy books lent themselves perfectly to secular distortion. But it was Ferdowsi who had, in the eleventh century, given the entire culture an identity and a voice. His sixty-thousand-couplet epic, the *Shahnameh*, which those in the West called *The Book of Kings*, had hymned a new Farsi into being, over the thirty years it took to complete, much as Shakespeare had sent more than fifteen hundred words and phrases into modern English.

We drew up at last at a marble edifice, at the far end of a quiet, formal garden in which couples dressed as for a restaurant in Paris were strolling around and posing for photos. We stepped into the chamber where the poet was buried, and Ali pointed out scenes from the epic poem rendered along the walls in friezes, while two romancing lovers pored over verses that warned of the capricious ways of Fate.

Then our driver slipped into the space behind us. He walked up to the sepulcher in which Ferdowsi's body was said to rest, and placed his hand on the cold stone. He took off his baseball cap and set it against his heart. Without preamble, in a rich and sonorous baritone, he proceeded to deliver a long sequence of verses from the poem that turns history into myth and vice versa.

Everything stopped. For what seemed like minutes we stood rapt.

I have made the world through a paradise of words.
No one has done that but me.
Huge palaces and monuments will fall into disrepair,
But I have made a palace out of words that shall never
    fade.
Through this I have immortalized Iran.

6

As Ali concluded his translation, the driver put on his cap once more and offered me a reassuring smile. "I didn't know if I could sing again," he explained, in perfect English. "Seven months ago I was diagnosed with cancer of the throat. My doctor advised me not to sing. But when I come here, I have to try. For Ferdowsi. For Iran."

———

A paradise of words: the driver's incantation might have been expressing the single most urgent impulse that had drawn me here. After years of travel, I'd begun to wonder what kind of paradise can ever be found in a world of unceasing conflict—and whether the very search for it might not simply aggravate our differences. And the natural place to embark upon such an inquiry—should we discard the notion of heaven entirely?—seemed to be the culture that had given us both our word for paradise and some of our most soulful images of it. The old Iranian term "Paradaijah" had been brought into Greek by Xenophon, when he'd served as a mercenary in Persia; and for centuries Persians, as most residents of Iran were then known, had cultivated detailed and ravishing visions of paradise in their walled gardens, as emblems of—enticements towards—the higher garden that awaits the fortunate.

The Magi who had traveled to Bethlehem to pay their

7

respects to the infant Jesus were often said to have come from Iran. So, too, the very word "magic" and the notion of a star shining above an auspicious birth. The water-softened courtyards that had bewitched me one candlelit evening in the Alhambra, the landscaped gardens depicting paradise around a marble tomb that had transfixed Hiroko and me on our honeymoon, at the Taj Mahal: all, I'd read, had been inspired by Persia.

But what gave particular power to the world's largest theocracy right now was that so many competing visions of paradise seemed to be crisscrossing every hour here, with furious intensity. After overthrowing the Shah and his Westward-facing regime in 1979, the ayatollahs who took over maintained that paradise awaits only those who give themselves to sacrifice and self-denial. The vast space in southern Tehran known as "Zahra's Paradise" was one of the largest cemeteries on earth—home to one and a half million dead bodies—and fast-track entry to heaven was said to be the privilege of martyrs.

Yet many of Iran's citizens were still known for the remarkably refined and sensuous versions of an earthly paradise they fashioned behind closed doors. The turbaned clerics, as they saw it, were ruthless politicians pursuing worldly ends under the guise of religion; the only pleasures that could be enjoyed in such a system lay in romance and intoxicants, the latest luxuries from abroad.

And both secular and religious souls, confoundingly, continued to turn for support to the Sufi poems that Iranian schoolchildren, to this day, learn by heart. Those mystical verses traffic in the language of the everyday—roses and nightingales and wine—if only to evoke a far deeper romance with the divine. Turning wordlessly in circles, Islamic dervishes incarnate a truth beyond doctrine and analysis.

Find a heaven within, Rumi had written—it came back to me now as Ali, the driver and I sat on a platform in the sun, munching on chicken with barberries—and you enter a garden in which "one leaf is worth more than all of Paradise."

Soon after we arrived back at our hotel, I fell into a deep sleep. By the time I awoke, darkness had fallen over Mashhad and I was hungry to experience the sacred city without my official guides.

I called Ali in his room and extended an invitation I knew he couldn't refuse. "Why don't you and the driver go to dinner alone? It looks really good."

"Are you sure?"

"I'm sure. I need to rest."

Then, true to the spirit of the culture all around me, I slipped down to the lobby and asked at the taxi desk if there was a car that could take me into the heart of town. Before long, a lean character of around thirty, with a boyish smile and unexpectedly good English, was leading me out to his battered compact.

"You have no friend?" he asked.

"I'm here in a group of one."

Holders of American passports were required to come in guided groups, but Iran was flexible about how this, like every term, might be interpreted.

"You come for the festival?"

"Festival?"

"This week," the driver explained. "The anniversary of Imam Reza." Five million people had gathered from every corner of the Shia world, he said—from Yemen and Pakistan and Beirut and Iraq, from all the provinces of Iran—to mark the auspicious occasion. Hence the archways of office buildings flooded in blue, the green lights under the trees that lined the sidewalks. Hence, too, perhaps, Ali's reluctance to allow me into the midst of passionate crowds.

The shrine of the imam, commemorating a holy man said to have been poisoned by an Iraqi rival almost twelve hundred years before, is believed to cure sickness and sorrow in every pilgrim who visits; an Iranian in California would later tell me that it was also now part of a massive cartel, a multinational corporation with land assets alone valued at twenty billion dollars. It ran fifty-six companies, including the only Coca-Cola plant in Iran.

As we pushed through a tiny entrance, behind a wall of bodies, all we could make out was celebration. On every side, people were seated on carpets under a huge moon. They were eating or chatting or, in some cases, stretched out asleep; many were spending seven days and seven nights in the mosque. There was a low roar of devotion, as of traffic on a busy street, and soon we were inside the roar ourselves.

Pilgrims were releasing white doves into the blue-black sky. Black-turbaned ayatollahs—direct descendants of the Prophet—were delivering sermons on huge video screens, under the pulsing moon. We picked our way between the illuminated blue-tiled buildings, and our feet could barely find space to touch the ground.

At last we came to the entrance to the holiest space of all, the innermost sanctum where the imam was buried, and my new friend looked over at me, assessingly. Nonbelievers were traditionally excluded from the entire complex, on pain of death; when the English traveler Robert Byron came to Mashhad in 1934, he blackened his face with burnt cork just to enter the outer courtyards of the shrine, then risked execution again by stealing in a second time. Yet I'd come all this way to see the complex, the driver clearly remembered, and my intentions appeared to be sincere; he gestured for me to accompany him inside.

Thrusting our way into a scrum of bodies again, we emerged within a very small room, thick with the smell of unwashed socks. The crowds here were so intense that little boys were being passed from shoulder to shoulder so they could arrive at the front and kiss the golden grille behind which lay the saint. A man wailed, and a great sound rose up around us. More than thirty million pieces of silver on the walls and chandeliers turned us all into a shiver of reflections.

I was humbled as I moved among the sobbing bodies. Men were running their hands down their faces and weeping as at their mother's funeral. More people pressed in, and the whole crowd seemed to sway and tremble, as if we were truly part of a single massed body. I'd lost contact by now with my driver, but then I caught sight of him across the room. His hand was on his heart, and he was stepping backwards, so as never to present his back to the long-dead holy man. His eyes were welling with tears.

We walked around the sacred space for a long, long time: rare privilege, perhaps, for both of us. As we passed back out into the courtyard, officials were circling around, waving blue and yellow and rainbow-colored feather dusters to prevent the press from turning into a mob. The great domes of the mosque shone against the full moon. We stepped in silence around pilgrims in the direction of the entrance and started making our slow way back to the parked car.

"I want a daughter!" the young driver suddenly exclaimed, opened up, perhaps, by the experience of visiting the saint. "So cute, with blond hair. I want a daughter just like my wife!"

"You'll be bringing your first child to the mosque?"

"My wife is in Yorkshire," he said, as if to remind a friend who knew this already. "She is in England, with her mother."

Noting my confusion, he went on, "I was going to the hospital in Sheffield, every day. To translate for my friend. I was talking to the nurse and then . . ."

A shy smile told the rest.

It had been several years now, he explained, since he'd fled Iran. He had researched the Schengen Agreement, so he knew he could get to the Netherlands. There he had made contact with a human trafficker and had paid the stranger twenty-five hundred dollars. The trafficker had led him to a truck and given him a special pipe through which he could breathe as he lay in the back, among five fellow stowaways from Afghanistan, hoping to escape detection by officials outside.

On arrival in Britain, he had been granted by the government both a solicitor and a translator. Free health care, too, and free housing and fifty pounds a week ("I spent just

THE HALF KNOWN LIFE

twenty!"). For three years the lawyer had petitioned a court on his behalf and finally he had been given asylum. Now he was free to reside in Britain for life.

"But you're back here?"

He nodded. "When I was in England, I was thinking about my people all the time. Sometimes, when I think of my family, the tears come out."

So, every summer, he stole back into Iran, to see his mother, his hometown, the mosque he could not forget. "In Europe," he went on, "I got onto this ship. It was, like, fifty meters high, like I'd seen in *Titanic*. I went to the first disco in my life there. On the fourth floor. Every day I'm going on the elevator to the swimming pool, to watch the sun rise. The first time I was at the pool, and I see all the women around with no clothes, I'm like, 'Omigod! Let's go swimming!' But after a month I felt like I was born in that place."

I asked more questions, as he steered us through streets alight with red and green neon, and found no discrepancies, no reasons for deceit. Only delight at his strange fortune and a kind of innocence.

"My heart was going boing-boing-boing," he said now, of entering the innermost recesses of the mosque. "I think Imam Reza gave me a blessing by bringing you here. Thanks to you, I came to Imam Reza on his birthday."

"You miss this place when you're away?" I asked, as we pulled up at the hotel, sounding foolish to myself.

He looked almost sheepish. "Even I am in England, I call my brother and ask him to go to the shrine and hold up the phone so I can feel it, hear it."

———

I couldn't sleep when I got back to my room. I had thought I knew something about Iran: twenty-eight years earlier, I'd financed my first book with a twenty-page article for the *Smithsonian* magazine, based on months of research, on the Assassin order in eleventh-century Iran, whose members committed murder under the assumption, wrote Marco Polo, they'd win a place in Paradise. Much later, I'd devoted four years to devouring everything I could find on the country to publish a long novel partly set in Iran, even though I'd never been there, and traveled from Damascus to Muscat to Sana'a and Beirut to absorb something of Islam today.

Now, however, within twenty hours, I was finding myself in the middle of something far richer than any of my ideas: a dissident risking his being to steal back into a land he'd risked his being to escape, and a deeply devoted Islamic soul—I'd witnessed with my own eyes—who did not wish to live in an Islamic republic.

It reminded me of the Iranian film I'd just seen, *A Separation*, which had possessed me as few films I could remember, though all its action, really, was internal. Every scene (in a straightforward-seeming story of a young couple in Tehran filing for divorce) disclosed a new detail or point of view that overturned the assumptions of the previous minute. There were so many sides to every question that one could not be sure of a thing or see how any issue could be resolved. It was like finding oneself inside the design of a carpet in which everything was in furious movement and yet the overall impression was one of unsettling calm.

That seemed to be the Iranian way: to undermine every certainty and recognize how every presumption was provisional. This sense of living on quicksand was surely deepened by the fact that six weeks earlier a new president had come to power—he was taking off now for New York to address the United Nations—but *A Separation* had suggested that even the long-running divorce between Iran and the West was never so clear-cut as it looked.

Ali, besides, seemed intent on reminding me how much in Iran remained beyond anyone's grasp. "For everyone," he'd said, as we were driving to Tus, "it's extremely difficult to assess what people think. So the people who come here thinking Iran is an enigma leave with an even richer sense of being puzzled." It had sounded like a pointed warning, much as his Calvin Klein watch and his constant talk of taking fellow Iranians on trips to Cape Town and Paris and Rio were a subtle reminder. Even the Supreme Leader, who had been guiding everything behind the scenes for almost twenty-five years, might not, he said, have a sense of what was going on, let alone of what would happen next.

I'd known before I arrived that Iran, with its many visions of heaven, would be sinuous and textured, a paradise of complications. But now I was having to make sense of heart-shaking, passionate displays of religious surrender from those who wished to have no part of religious rule. I was having to navigate a world in which the Association of Combatant Clerics was a liberal, reformist group, and the Combatant Clergy Association an opposing, rightist one. I had to remember how even divorce was not just a private affair, as the government was working to push the country back to traditional Islamic practice—a man could leave his wife just by saying "I divorce you" three times in the presence of two witnesses—while its more independent-minded citizens were sending divorce rates surging, with highly educated women reclaiming rights often denied them.

The beauty of films like *A Separation*, I realized, is that they hold you for two hours with supple and constant swerves, and at the end you're farther from a clear conclusion than ever.

When finally he agreed to take me on an official tour of the central shrine in Mashhad—now the festival was over—Ali led me to one of its museums, and pointed out a double-edged sword. This was a Persian invention, he asserted with pride. As was the decimal fraction, as well as the game of chess. He took pains, I noted, not to say whether it was violence that was double-edged or its suppression.

Decades earlier, I'd moved to Japan in part because it was the most inward and subtle culture I'd met: the relation of surface to depth remains beguilingly uncertain there and I can never begin to imagine I can get to the bottom of things. Yet my neighbors around Kyoto hold on to their privacy by saying little and expressing, with their faces, even less; here in Iran I was surrounded by some of the most articulate souls I'd ever met, and the more they said, the less I could tell where they stood. Or where I did. The culture that had officially invented Paradise seemed a treasure house of riddles.

This didn't make me unhappy. As a boy I'd been taught to cherish knowledge till I became impossibly eager to parade my knowingness, as if I were on top of everything I saw. But the older I got, the more I realized how much existed beyond my plans and expectations. I felt in my bones what even the general and president Ulysses S. Grant, in the second sentence of his memoirs, had observed: "There are but few important events in the affairs of men brought about by their own choice." Recognizing how much lay beyond my knowledge was what made space for growth and surprise, and kept me usefully in place.

We all know the fact of death, I sometimes reminded myself, but that seems of little use until you struggle to find breath; we soon know the facts of life, but those have little value until you've tasted them firsthand. So long as I was in the thick of things, I felt—more and more—less like a master of the universe than its servant. And I knew that Iran's poets echoed what I'd read in the wise, anonymous fourteenth-century guide to clear living, *The Cloud of Unknowing*: "By our love, the divine may be reached and held; by our thinking, never."

As we touched down at our next stop, Kerman—disembarking from a spotless Airbus A300, whose pilot had delivered his announcements in impeccable English—I wanted to see how the government might put the idea of paradise to use in some way different from its poets. Ali was eager to show me the thirteenth-century bazaar, where pistachios come with shells within shells. But I'd spotted something more intriguing along the streets: a classical Persian palace encircled by a lavish garden, with two pavilions facing the main road.

The sign outside declared "Museum of Holy Defense," and I guessed it must commemorate the trench conflict of the 1980s, in which Iran and Iraq had fought one another, over eight years, to a stalemate, leaving one million people dead. I asked Ali if we could go in, so as to learn more about the beardless boys who stared back at me from every other lamppost: "martyrs" from that decades-old war who, often barely in their teens, ran towards enemy guns with plastic keys around their necks to open the doors to Paradise.

Inside the sumptuous mansion—it could have belonged to a French president—I was again reminded how everything I thought I knew looked different on the far side of the world; I might have been peering through a kaleidoscope that was being constantly shaken. In Iran the war was seen not just as an opportunistic land grab by Saddam Hussein, aware that an inexperienced-seeming clergy had come to power nearby; it was yet another tragedy caused by Western interference. It was American intelligence, I read in one of the museum's English-language captions, that directed Saddam's chemical weapons. It was French allies who sent the Iraqis Mirage fighter-bombers. It was Soviets who provided Saddam with advisers and tanks, along with missiles.

This was the same lesson I'd learned when turning on the TV in Mashhad, to see that the "war in Syria" was here, on the local English-language channel, a "war on Syria." The only way past such differences seemed to be contained in the two chaste tombs outside the museum, and perhaps the universal spirit with which five women, dressed from head to toe in black, sat in the September sunshine and read in silence from their copies of the Koran.

The inner Iran, which I'd excavated through poems, had given me some of the most intimate depictions I'd encountered of how to make contact with the divine; poets really could be the unacknowledged legislators of the world in a culture where taxi drivers recite mystical verses and ayatollahs speak in double-edged stanzas.

But poetry is the form that shimmers between fact and fiction, a world of suggestions that does not allow one to settle into certainties. I went up to my room after a long day of dialectics with my enigmatic companion, and was reminded in a local English-language daily that Facebook was technically banned in Iran, for reasons of "health." I happened to know it had seventeen million users here. My own AOL account, through which I'd eagerly sent emails home on connections in the holy city faster than the one I'd had in California, now threw off messages in Farsi every time I opened my laptop, and rainbowed boxes telling me it was blocked. I could walk downstairs, however, whenever I chose and log on to the hotel computer with ease.

As I got ready to sleep, I remembered how the devout driver who had taken me to the central shrine my first evening here had, when we arrived back at my hotel, refused to take payment for his four hours of showing me around.

"Please," I said.

"No!" he protested. "This is friendship."

"I know. But this is your job as well."

"No. It is my honor. How can I charge a guest?"

At last I pushed some of the money into his hand, knowing full well that he would feel cheated—and suffer—if I didn't. My research had reminded me of the custom of ta'arof, or never saying exactly what you mean, and three-part refusals. But I'd barely guessed, when reading of Iran, how hard it might be in life to tell where custom ends and conviction begins.

————

When I'd encountered accounts of the Garden of Eden as a boy, I'd always been encouraged by the transparency they ascribed to the walled paradise; one feature of the Garden seemed to be that light and dark are very clearly defined, and its artless residents know exactly which tree is forbidden, which not. Here in the land of embroidered interiors, however, everything was in shadow and in constant motion. The judgments of God are seldom so ambiguous as those of the men who say they are speaking on behalf of God.

"Iranian architecture is introvert," I heard as I walked one hot morning around the deserted citadel at Rayen, its sun-dried brick looming in front of mountains that soar to higher than thirteen thousand feet. "Because you're living in a harsh environment—and also for reasons of security. You don't want to be open to the world." My guide might also have noted that ninety percent of the people around me were Shia; as a distinct minority in Islam for thirteen hundred years, they had long been given license to dissemble, if only to ensure their survival.

Yet this centuries-old reverence for the "unseen life" had taken on new implications in a surveillance culture in which the government was constantly trying to find out what its people were thinking and its people were permanently trying to divine what their government was up to. Watchfulness on both sides had stretched even wider the gulf between what was said and what was felt. I sensed I'd ended up inside a chess game in which both sides were mostly using their knights, moving two squares back and one to the side, or two squares to the side and then one square back.

One evening we heard that the new president was giving a rare—a critical—press conference in New York. We gathered around a TV and, almost instantly, the broadcast cut out. A technical glitch or a form of censorship? Nobody could tell.

Next day, Ali and I were speeding again through the desert, on a modern superhighway that might have been cutting towards Palm Springs, stopping off at a many-chambered caravanserai that represented the country's latest entry in the boutique hotel market, passing the uranium enrichment plant that had long been an object of furious global speculation. Of course a desert culture would always see an explosion of greenery and running water as a kind of salvation, I thought; paradise gardens are a flood of color and fertility in a world of dust and heat.

In Yazd, the Silk Road desert town associated with Zoroastrianism, we traveled out to the temple where a flame had been burning continuously, so it was said, for more than fifteen hundred years. It spoke for an ancient tradition that had given the world our sense of heaven and hell, of angels, even of the Day of Judgment. Yet it was far from the official sights, back in the hotel, that I was truly transformed. One evening I stepped out into its water-singing gardens and found myself in a fairyland of colored lights. Divans had been set up on which soft-eyed couples were exchanging murmurs, while sweet music drifted through the fragrant dark. I slipped off my shoes, lay back, and was treated to slices of watermelon and cups of strong tea in what felt more like heaven on earth than anywhere I'd met.

In the oasis city of Shiraz, the transport deepened as I went out before breakfast to the park next to our hotel; a blond woman in full chador was laughingly driving past her boyfriend in a one-on-one game on a basketball court. Lovers were paddling palms in leafy corners. Along the streets billboards with English translations declared, "Verily, Allah does not love any self-conceited boaster," but that did not seem to deter a teenager with plucked eyebrows I would see strutting past in a T-shirt that announced, "ONLY GOD CAN JUDGE" and then, in tiny letters, "me."

The central sight in the city is the tomb of the poet Hafez, and when I went there in the warm dusk, students were lining up to offer prayers to the alabaster shrine. One by one, each of them stepped up to the pillared dome to open a thick copy of the poet's verses, from almost seven hundred years before; on the basis of the lines they chanced upon, they would make the critical decisions of their lives. Should I marry? Should my beloved take on robes? Should we attempt to flee? Outside the garden's gates, a trained bird was picking out cards to dispense other futures.

Hafez's poems of drunkenness and love had always been impeccably double-edged; but when holy men deliberated over whether his dead body belonged in heaven or hell, they opened a book of the poet's, at random, and came upon a classic Sufi koan: "Though drowned in sin, Heaven is his lot."

Like many a mystic, Hafez professed to have no interest in names or distinctions: he was neither Christian nor Hindu nor Muslim nor Buddhist nor Jew, this teacher of Koranic studies wrote in one celebrated poem; heaven was the place where such divisions fell away. Nowadays, far from this romantic garden (which once included a cemetery), the ever-unreadable Islamic Republic reserved one seat in parliament for a representative from the Assyrian community, another for a member of the Jewish community and another for a Zoroastrian, though all such minorities were famously persecuted. Iran remained home to the largest Jewish population in the Middle East outside of Israel, and it was Zoroastrianism that had given it the first gardens that served as a mirror of something more lasting.

When we arrived in Qom, the spiritual center of Iran, where sixty thousand seminarians from around the globe study dialectics not far from where Ayatollah Khomeini lived in a mud-and-straw house, Ali led me into the "Foreign Pilgrims' Office" to see if I could gain permission to enter the main shrine. A warm-eyed official handed me an elegant English-language brochure and bustled off to fetch me some peach juice and cookies.

By his side a young cleric with intense, dark eyes started making small talk that did not seem so small. "You are American? Where do your parents come from? Do you have relations with the Iranian community in California?"

The friendly official led me to the innermost chamber of the shrine—I still didn't know how (or whether) I had passed the test—and we saw men rocking back and forth in prayer, tears streaming down their cheeks, while a group of others, all in black, carried a silver coffin across the courtyard outside to receive the blessing of a saint.

On arrival back in my hotel, I opened the booklet the official had given me and found it rich with advice about being on guard: "Keep your money in hidden pockets." I recalled the booklet I'd been given in the great mosque at Mashhad, bearing the unexpected title "Techniques and Rules of Friendship." Inside, it had advised me, "Do not trust a friend before testing him." Also, "One should not reveal his and his relatives' secrets to someone just because of friendship."

Mirrors are cherished in Persian architecture, I recalled, because they suggest an infinity of reflections, something one can never get to the end of. Islamic art regularly attempts to suggest the divine through elaborate patterning, a kind of geometry. Yet as I found myself lost in the reduplicating visions, I started, as never before in a lifetime of travel, to look over my shoulder. I began tearing up articles in my carry-on that, if read in the wrong light, could seem less innocent than they really were. I took to writing emails to myself, sometimes in code, offering rhapsodic tributes to the country around me. The farther I went in Iran, as perhaps in life, the more I was having to surrender.

My last night in the country, I was eager to meet the niece of an Iranian friend in California; I presented my request to Ali and he looked pained. "Please," he said, "we ask that you do not visit any private homes. Perhaps you can meet your friend in the lobby of the hotel?" He didn't need to remind me that the Laleh Hotel is famous for its bugs; most of the people in the lobby looked to be neither guests nor staff.

I had no intention of getting my long-suffering and law-abiding guide in trouble, so I arranged to meet the niece in the lobby. I placed myself in a chair facing the front door, recalling that it was strictly forbidden in the Islamic Republic even to shake hands with the opposite sex.

When a pair of smiling women in their midforties came in, confident and chic, one of them caught my eye, waved a hello and led her friend towards me with warm hands extended, seemingly ready to enfold me in a hug. I told them I'd been asked not to set foot in their homes, and they whisked me off to a stylish vegetarian restaurant in a cutting-edge arts center.

"Is it okay?" I asked.

"What is not okay?" said one of my new friends, large eyes flashing.

We passed through a bookshop filled with DVDs of the documentary *War Photographer* and books with titles in English—*Situating Salsa*—and came out into a restaurant where we could settle in over corn-and-tomato pizzas. One of the women was a playwright and director, and explained, "In the theater it's difficult, because everything is so—er, moody. You start a project and you don't know what the position will be tomorrow. Even they send someone to observe your work—everything is 'under observation'—and they say it's okay. Then, when you're finished, they say you can't show it, and everything is gone—your time, your money."

There had been a battle, I learned, over whether live music could be played during a production of *Uncle Vanya*. Yet a seventeen-year-old Iranian woman had sent a film to Cannes about the incarceration of twelve-year-old girls in her country, titled, rather pregnantly, *The Apple*. To be "protected" from temptation, she might have been saying, was only to become dangerously defenseless before it.

Still, there was no point in complaining, both women agreed. "Every country has its difficulties," said one. "You have to accept it. Because what can you do?"

Many young people, she went on, were living in sin.

"It isn't forbidden?"

"Yes," she said, large eyes growing even larger. "Yes, it is forbidden! But they do it, they find a way." I noticed how it was these women involved in the world of make-believe— the director's friend was an actor—who seemed more forthcoming and unguarded than anyone I'd met here. I also remembered how, when I'd looked up the origin of the double-edged sword back in my hotel, the first example I'd found, from the Merriam-Webster dictionary, had read, "This much freedom of expression and opinion can be a double-edged sword."

Not long before, I'd been worried about how—or whether—I was going to leave the country the following day. Many a foreigner feels a tap on the shoulder at the final checkpoint in the airport and realizes, too late, that he's been given a visa only so he can lead government agents towards dissidents or informers. Once, on a balmy California evening, I'd enjoyed an invigorating conversation with a young Iranian American man about how writing can build a bridge between cultures that too often see one another only through projections. Some years later, my new friend, Jason Rezaian, then writing for *The Washington Post*, found himself held for 544 days in a Tehran prison, apparently for trying to see both of his homelands with compassion.

Now, though, the two women were speaking about Al Pacino and Antigone, about Peter Brook and Daniel Day-Lewis. A friend of theirs hoped to be part of the country's celebrated film world, but it was difficult. "He likes John Woo. Tarantino, Jim Jarmusch. It's not easy to make such films in Iran."

"You must always remember that word 'moody,'" the theater director said, pushing her light brown hair under her headscarf.

"Do many people want to leave?"

"All," she said. "It is like a utopia for them," she went on, of the country her government still took pains to insult. "Traveling to the United States, where everything is possible."

"It's human nature, don't you think? The place you haven't seen is heaven."

"I don't think so," said the other, dark eyes blazing once again. "When I was young, we were not exposed to other places. We did not know about them. Maybe some people dreamed of coming to Tehran. Now all the world is a small village."

"A small village in which we know so little about our neighbors."

Then the phone rang, and we had to bring our conversation to a halt because it was her brother, calling from London.

———

I packed very carefully when I got back to my room. I checked my passport again; I did what I could to conceal my notes, and wrote "Paradise," instead of "Iran," all over them. On top I placed the brochures I'd received in the mosque, featuring "Techniques and Rules of Friendship." I thought of the poor hack in some basement who had been deputed to read my emails, which had grown ever more effusive in their raptures about the Islamic Republic. I also remembered the evening when Ali and I had driven through the intensely crowded streets of Yazd, cars darting in from every direction at high speed as pedestrians wandered in front of hurtling buses. In many places, the all-against-all traffic here had the terrifying chaos of India. Yet with far fewer horns, so the impression was of cool menace, with no thought of the country's twenty thousand road deaths a year.

"Here in Iran," Ali had said from the front seat, turning around to look me in the eye, "we don't give way. We take way." He wasn't speaking only of traffic, I knew. "But it's constantly based on psychology. You're always assessing how naive or crazy the other guy is, and making lightning decisions as to whether to surge forward or hold back." Then he turned around again, so I was faced with his back, in a country where every road came with speed bumps, and everyone had her own idea about whether this was the way to paradise, or to somewhere rather different.

The Promised Land

I couldn't get Iran out of my mind after I flew away—or maybe it was out of some deeper part of my being. Not just because of its rich ambiguities, its lacquered beauty and the iron presence I always sensed hovering over that beauty; but most of all because of the way it constantly shimmered a little out of reach, leaving me wondering whether the longing for an ideal world might not be a kind of curse, even a heresy.

This wasn't an abstract issue: sometimes it could feel like the story of my life. Every time Ali spoke about his days at school near London, I flashed back to my own time in a place not many miles away, in exactly the same era. Two hundred acres of green fields in which we could lose ourselves in wandering every afternoon; long games of tennis in the golden light of summer evenings; conversations in our little cells for hours after midnight on the meaning of the universe and all the loves and lives that surely awaited us.

To an outsider, I knew, our days at school could look as circumscribed—as strictly supervised—as the ones I'd seen in Tehran; a cane was always at the ready in the headmaster's study and we had to dance attention on older boys as if we were their footmen in some ancient war. Bells tolled us to class before the light came up and we were sent on long runs through winter sludge, fording rivers and tramping through bogs as beasts of burden might. In the mornings we had to compose poems in dead languages; in the evenings, to recite the Lord's Prayer in Latin.

Almost every tree was forbidden in our world, and not a single Eve was in sight. "Dream not of other worlds," we heard the angel tell Adam in the religious epic we were obliged to read, *Paradise Lost*. "Be lowly wise: think only what concerns thee, and thy being." We weren't even allowed to walk along one side of the main road that ran through our little town. Why? Because someone in the 530-year history of the school had deemed that freedom is best learned by mastering restraint.

And yet, when I left, I had a haunting sense of the gates of Eden swinging shut behind me. We'd been protected in our walled garden from most of the convulsions of the world—and from the turmoil in many a family, often especially acute when teenage boys are running wild. Instead, we'd found ourselves in the hands of men who had one skill in life, and that was the taming of adolescent males.

Three times a year, after seventy or eighty days in the cloister—struggling to parse Xenophon and imbibing an Old Testament creed of obedience and discipline—I flew back to my parents' yellow house in the hills of California, where all the revolutions of the 1960s were exploding around us. Whatever was unknown, it was felt, had to be better than what was known and found to be imperfect. Sweep aside the past, and a bright new future could shine through.

It was a glorious youthful efflorescence and my parents were in the thick of it. Back in England, my friends and I longed to be in the Far West with its fresh liberations and wide blue horizons, its Summer of Love; we devoured the latest bulletins from the Revolution—the Dead, Hunter Thompson, *Rolling Stone*—and felt that anything must be possible in the new world that was being sung into life.

As time went on, however, I began to wonder whether the changes all around me in Santa Barbara arose out of need as much as hope. The idealistic kids who burned down the bank ten minutes from our house seemed almost to be yearning for the stability of tradition, the warmth of community, even protective elders to stand in the place of the parents whom they were, in many senses, missing.

So back and forth I went, every three months for more

than a decade, between the wide-open horizons of a per-
petual future and the walled certainties of custom-bound
tradition. Between hope and history, as it could seem. One
day I was donning a surplice over my morning dress to
march in solemn formation down the nave of the quasi cathedral across our cobblestoned courtyard; the next, I was
trying to coax my hair out from behind my ears as I prepared to drive up to Telegraph Avenue.

As soon as I came of age, I posted myself full-time in the
New World, and started inhaling the gospel of possibility as
it came to me through Emerson and Thoreau. Why look to
old Europe and the wisdom of conventions? they reminded
me: we are wiser than we know, if only we can awaken to a
sense of all that lies beyond our knowledge. "Shams and de-
lusions are esteemed for soundest truths," Thoreau had pro-
nounced, twenty minutes from where I was reading those
words, "while reality is fabulous."

But was humanity really progressing in a straight line,
as technology sometimes seemed to do? And didn't giddy
expectations lead to disappointments, of precisely the kind
the young don't know what to do with? The pursuit of
happiness made deepest sense, I came to think, when seen
in the framework of the Eastern awareness that suffering is
the first truth of existence. Adam and Eve had to quit Eden
if only so they could learn to resist the lure of serpents.
Much as the young prince who became the Buddha had to

quit his golden palace in order to confront the facts of sickness and old age and death. A true paradise has meaning only after one has outgrown all notions of perfection and taken the measure of the fallen world.

So I left endless summer to travel into a world of autumn: a single room on the backstreets of Kyoto, Japan's eighth-century capital, where people had been living for more than a thousand years with the knowledge that reality is neither an insult nor an aberration, but the partner with whom we have to make our lives. Meanwhile, forces far beyond me kept disclosing plans of their own, which had little to do with my own tiny hopes. One evening my family home back in California burned to the ground and I lost every last thing I'd ever acquired, not least the handwritten notes that might have made up my next three books. Eight months on, I drove out of the rubble of my life, three hours up the coast, and stepped into a sunlit room in a hermitage that opened a door to a paradise of clarity I hadn't allowed myself to believe in.

I went to South Korea and held my breath while tens of thousands of devotees raised their arms and chanted in unison at open-air evangelical services; at night, the skyline of Seoul looked like a field of illuminated crosses. I traveled again and again to the controlled societies of Cuba and Burma and China, to see if a collective utopia could ever make space for the fact that each of us has a very different sense of what a life of purpose and beauty might look like. And then, in 1990, I finally made it to North Korea, the "People's Paradise," where people seemed a little beside the point and perfection was seen as simply the ruthless elimination of every last imperfection.

I needed to go there because I wanted to see what a whole nation built around a secular faith might look like. "Intentional communities" had been all the rage when I was growing up, and it made sense that a community fashioned with intent would have more coherence—more integrity—than one backed into, or haphazardly improvised. Yet a circle nearly always seemed to need a center and that center—generally a leader or a doctrine—was unlikely to prove infallible.

As I wandered around the planet-shaped halls and car-less streets of Pyongyang, I found myself within a world as tightly sealed as any I had encountered; in most dictatorships I'd visited, the locals would do everything they could to make contact with foreigners, their best hope for contraband ideas and plans of escape. In North Korea, citizens crossed the road every time they saw me approach. It was sobering to realize that not a word I said, when I started to hold forth on "universal truths" and our shared reality, began to apply to the people I saw around me here.

If the Age of Globalism could leave us ever more provincial, the Age of Information seemed to leave us knowing less about the rest of the world than ever before—and least of all about the places we heard most about. My friends and I could recite a few broad sound bites about the nuclear policies of Pyongyang or Tehran, their war-threatening leaders, their shattered economies. But the more we got secondhand, the farther we were from real life. Somehow it seemed easier than ever to sit in a darkened cave, backs turned to the world, hypnotized by images projected on the walls that keep reality at a distance.

My most striking moment on that first trip to North Korea had begun when my guide had led me up to the top of a hill, our last day together. We'd come to know one another quite well, since he was seldom more than a few feet away from me, and I was traveling in a group of one; he'd tasted the larger world as a student for three years in Pakistan. But his time outside the streamlined surfaces of the "Workers' Paradise" had left him unconvinced that anarchy was truly any better than stage-managed perfection.

"Don't repeat my propaganda," he'd said, as he invited me to look across the gleaming high-rises of a city that, thirty-seven years before, had seen three buildings in every four destroyed amid the devastations of the Korean War. "Just tell your friends what you saw and thought and felt here." North Korea was terrifying to me because its people really did know so little of the outside world; it's always easiest to launch a nuclear missile against an abstraction.

39

But as I returned home, I wondered if those of us dwelling in seeming freedom know any more about North Korea—even though we don't have the excuse of a government that refuses to let us leave our hometowns, or one that will execute us for so much as a glance at a foreign newspaper.

———

One warm summer day, I found myself, with my wife, in Belfast. The official reason for our visit was improbable: a literary festival organized by some friends on behalf of Jaipur, the northern India town that had quickly, in our overturning world, become home to the planet's most exhilarating celebration of writing. Troubled places often look to writers in the hope that imagination can see beyond the divisions that ideologies enforce; the writer's job, after all, is to dismantle the very notion of an Other by showing how your hurts belong to me, as my hopes do to you.

For someone like myself, growing up in England in the 1960s and 1970s, Northern Ireland had long been the war next door; we might hear vague rumors about Cambodia and Uganda, but this was our very own Jerusalem, whose sectarian walls and bloody explosions brought violence to our doorsteps daily. One moment a car bomb was exploding in London, setting off a sheet of flames forty feet high and stripping a nearby policeman of his uniform; the next, a bomb was killing the last viceroy of India, Lord Mount-batten, along with a boy who had just graduated from our elementary school. Everyone I knew had an opinion on "the Troubles," in part because nobody I knew had actually been to Northern Ireland; the Falls Road, Londonderry, the Shankill became the cursed names we grew up with, and onto which we projected our most lurid fears.

The minute Hiroko and I stepped out of the airport terminal in Belfast, we were greeted by a red-faced man, quite beefy, who looked gratifyingly close to the Northern Ireland of stereotype. He drove us into the unexpectedly small town, on this sunny day in mid-June, and told us that all the latest visitors, from China, loved to visit the monument to where the *Titanic* had been built, just before the "Ship of Dreams" sailed into a crushing reality. Others flocked to Titanic Studios, the quixotically named film production facility where *Game of Thrones* was shot. In the age of streaming, Belfast had become an ever more popular home to fairy tale and romance.

We drew closer to the Holiday Inn, and suddenly we were at the entrance to a small bridge on the narrow road. Just over there, the driver said, was the enemy side. People didn't like to go there. Nor did the people from over there like to come back across this modest thoroughfare. A Sean over here would have to become "Sam" once he got to the other side. It was a small town, so people knew one another; they could tell if you were so-and-so's son—or if you were the so-and-so who'd helped abduct a neighbor, an impoverished widow and mother of ten, thirty-six years before.

On the far side of the bridge, banners stretched across the road celebrating Donald Trump, above cardboard cutouts of the Queen. One group here associated itself with the Palestinians, and in time we'd see signs from the other side scrawled up in Hebrew script. Everything was a pretext for division, and I remembered how even the North Korean movie *Nameless Heroes* had taken pains to include an Irishman aggrieved about the occupation of his country.

Like many an ill-starred place, this spiritual home of civil war had realized that its best hope for revival might be to make a killing out of its bad name. To offer visitors a sense of history here was to focus on the conflicts outsiders heard so much about, and I sometimes wondered whether the locals, not unlike the people of North Korea, were acting out their animosities the way others might portray princesses along Disneyland's Main Street. Our first morning in Belfast we took a "Black Cab" tour, in which our driver went out of his way to broadcast his hatred—he recited a whole litany of children killed before he had even turned on the ignition—and then gave us a furiously partisan view of the Sinn Fein stations of the cross. Hiroko's eyes filled with tears and I reminded her that the drivers two blocks away had stories of their own. In the afternoon we went to the Crumlin Road Gaol, where we were invited to marry our kids off in a facility where "seventeen men have been executed." If we'd had time, we could have taken in a "History of Terror" tour to the site of Bloody Friday—almost two dozen bombs exploding in barely an hour—and the homes of terrorists.

Belfast had grown expert at playing itself, as if its livelihood depended on it. The Sunday of our visit, however, we woke up early, on what was almost the longest day of the year, and headed out—as perhaps others were preparing for church—to the grimy, beat-up residential streets of the industrial east.

We stepped out of the double-decker bus at C. S. Lewis Square—the celebrated man of God had enjoyed a front-seat view on the quarrels of faith, growing up here—and looked around the flat, grubby neighborhood. Then we handed over a pound for a map and followed a trail through the featureless community.

Turning off the main road, we passed a leafy street with relatively big houses along it. A sign announced "Cyprus Avenue."

"Stop!" I cried to Hiroko. "You've got to take my picture here."

She was startled; in thirty-one years together, I'd never made such a request.

"It reminds you of the street where you grew up, in Oxford?"

"No, no." I shook my head, impatient. "I'll explain it to you later."

We walked down to a place called St. Donard's Church, where people had gathered in a small parking lot to flog unwanted stuff out of the backs of cars; a friendly woman with the doughy, pale face I'd long associated with Belfast sold Hiroko a pair of turquoise earrings for a third the price of a bar of chocolate. Then we continued for a few more blocks until we came to a black sign that said "Hyndford Street" and headed down a row of identical redbrick terraced houses to where a humble plaque, barely visible, announced that two weeks after World War II concluded, Van Morrison had been born in this grim building.

An old woman across the street refused to respond to Hiroko's friendly call of hello. I demanded another photo. We headed round the corner to the primary school the snarling Transcendental singer had attended, and went down to "the Hollow," familiar to everyone who's ever sung or heard "Brown Eyed Girl."

"I've never seen you like this," said Hiroko.

"This is the landscape I've been walking through, in my head, for thirty years," I reminded her. "Sunday six-bells. Orangefield. Beechie River." All the everyday boyhood places out of which Van Morrison had made a scripture.

I couldn't find the words for it exactly, but out of this bleak set of row houses, in a city known for brutality, the lonely only child listening to Radio Luxembourg and the African American singers of the Delta had fashioned heavenly transports. He'd made of the unpromising landscape a world as magically illuminated as Avalon. In earliest childhood, Morrison believed, lie memories of some purer world, the people we were before the Fall. So it was only by going back, "way, way, way back," to somewhere "previous"—this clenched and ugly neighborhood, as it was for him—that he could retrieve some ancient vision that had been lost.

This could all sound like wishfulness—unforgivable romance—except that between every slow anthem about "the Garden," Van recorded ill-tempered sing-alongs in which he announced that he wasn't feeling it no more, railed against fans calling for heaven on demand, trilled that there's "no rhyme or reason, no master plan, no Nirvana, no Promised Land." He was more than ready to give cheerful voice to the fact that nothing lasts for long. Yet the very fact he could see any light at all in such broken streets, in a city defined by divisions, was a moving reassurance.

We spent an enraptured hour wandering around the terrain that had given the Belfast singer intimations of the beautiful world he'd passed on to so many of us. A few minutes later, we were back among the "Peace Walls" that spoke for an ongoing war.

My trip to East Belfast had been a kind of pilgrimage, I realized after I left, to a place that had held my imagination for half a lifetime. Seeing the streets whose names I could recite like a secular prayer confirmed a hope inside me, in part because everything around them was so stubbornly unvarnished. The North Road Bridge, the Castlereagh hills, all the places that had come to me from afar existed in the midst of a very tough reality. Van hadn't been fleeing the difficult circumstances of his life so much as working to find in them the lost pearl of something better.

Yet how could the people around him possibly find transcendence when ninety percent of their kids still attended segregated schools and neighbors kept talking about reviving the war? How make sense of the words of a local priest—he lived in a monastery at just the place where Catholic streets met Protestant—that "you find God in the midst of the Troubles"? And how keep faith with even the hope of Paradise when nearly all the paradises I'd seen were, sometimes for that very reason, war zones?

One year after my trip to Iran, I was back in North Korea, intent on seeing the land of projections through its film industry. The showpiece capital had always struck me as a massive stage set, all Legoland skyscrapers and false fronts. Most of the glittery high-rises were said to be ghost towers, cousins to the completely empty fake town built at the DMZ. Even now, the blue-glass, 105-story Ryugyong Hotel, shaped like a rocket ship—the largest tourist hotel in the world for a land that saw barely four thousand non-Chinese tourists a year—remained "under construction," as it had been twenty-four years before. Still the government continued to screen its citizens from all other realities, in the hope that they might believe theirs to be the best of all possible worlds.

I'd picked up on my first trip, from shelves packed with works by the Kims, the 329-page tract the country's second leader, Kim Jong Il, had published called *On the Art of the Cinema*; in this, as on so many fronts, he'd taken Lenin's ideas about cinema as a propaganda tool and executed them to the last chilling degree. As I wandered around the Pyongyang Film Studios, three times larger than the Paramount lot in Hollywood, I was reminded that the second Kim had "guided" 11,890 projects here. He was widely believed to have owned the largest private video library in the world, more than twenty thousand titles strong; in his eagerness to boost the local film industry, he had famously abducted a celebrated South Korean actress in Hong Kong, and then her former husband, a director.

Everyone was onstage in North Korea, even we foreign visitors, who were so often spies or missionaries or journalists, traveling under false pretenses. When I entered one of the city's subway cars, far from the movie studio, after descending a spotless escalator into a world of murals and golden statues, a local leaned over and smiled, before asking me, in perfect English, "Are you enjoying your trip?" An actor, I had to assume, planted by the government to leave a good impression.

Yet I'd come here again because I refused to believe that humanity could ever be entirely suppressed; at some point, surely, it has to peek out from behind the gates of ideology. One morning, I noticed a white Chanel clip in the hair of our spirited and strikingly presentable guide, Miss Lee (as I'll call her); two members of our group offered to show her *Frozen* on an iPad, and she confessed that she knew "Let It Go" already since she'd seen the film. One of her colleagues—an amiable young character who'd serenaded us with a heartfelt rendition of "Danny Boy"—learned that two in our circle worked for Apple and, in the safety of our minivan, leaned forwards to ask how Tim Cook's management style differed from that of Steve Jobs. She had such a good job, said Miss Lee, working every day with foreigners, but one consequence was that she had so little time to date. Now, at twenty-six, she was becoming an old maid.

Was this a line she'd been told to deliver? It was impossible to tell. Were our handlers aware enough of other possibilities to crave a different kind of paradise? In Japan my neighbors are generally quite content to play their parts, impeccably, in the orchestrated pantomime that is public life, if it will help sustain a safe, clean, smoothly running harmony from which almost everyone can benefit. But my friends in Japan remain as brightly colored, as passionate, often, within their homes as they are self-effacing in the street; in North Korea I couldn't guess at how much private life might be possible behind closed doors. It was easy to suspect that, as in Cuba, a man might be wary of expressing doubts even to his wife.

"In the soul of man," Herman Melville wrote, in one of his terrifying flights of prophecy in *Moby-Dick*, "there lies one insular Tahiti, full of peace and joy, but encompassed by all the horrors of the half known life." Cast off from that protected world, he'd gone on, and "thou canst never return!"

But the half known life is where so many of our possibilities lie. In the realm of worldly affairs it can be a tragedy that so many of us in our global neighborhood choose to see other places through screens, reducing fellow humans to two dimensions. On a deeper level, however, it's everything half known, from love to faith to wonder and terror, that determines the course of our lives. Melville's sorrow lay not just in his restless inquiries, but in his hope for answers in a world that seems always to simmer in a state of answerlessness.

Should we resign ourselves then to the conviction that

nothing can get better? My days in Belfast had brought back to me the verses of the local poet Seamus Heaney. When he'd seen Nelson Mandela released from prison after twenty-seven years, the man who'd witnessed so many of the Troubles dared to believe that sometimes longed-for possibilities really can come true. Inspired by that moment, he'd written the now celebrated lines, in an adaptation of a Sophocles play about the Trojan War, "Once in a lifetime . . . hope and history rhyme." Heaney's life in Belfast had shown him, every hour, how brutally history mocks hope; yet he was wise enough to know that a life that doesn't know possibility takes in only half the truth.

———

One warm afternoon in Isfahan, I'd actually walked through the pavilion of Eight Paradises—or so the name of the Hasht Behesht palace suggests. As Ali and I wandered around the octagonal structure, all mirror-work and crystal domes, he handed me a poem by Omar Khayyam, the master of geometry whose verses had become a scripture for my parents, as for the Brits who governed them. It was a verse that seemed designed to deny one any hope of shelter.

Some are thoughtful on their way,
Some are doubtful, so they pray.

I hear the hidden voice that may
Shout, "Both paths lead astray."

Then, as we walked towards the Garden of Nightingales, he passed along another set of verses, which I absorbed slowly in the sun as we walked among the trees.

The secrets eternal neither you know nor I,
And answers to the riddle neither you know nor I,
Behind the veil there is much talk about us, why
When the veil falls, neither you remain nor I.

Such a bracing call to submission! Not only could we hope to know next to nothing, but our lives would be determined, perhaps, by what we did with all we didn't know. It reminded me a little of how the searching Cistercian monk Thomas Merton regularly confessed in his letters that the only faith he could trust would be the one that came to him not as an answer but as a probably unanswerable question.

On the Lake

Kashmir was the local paradise that bewitched my cousins all across India. The mountainous region in the country's far north was, for them, the home of otherwise unthinkable snowballs, of golden fields of mustard, of peaks to rival the ones they'd read of in the Alps. Whenever they went to the cinema in their congested cities, they were apt to see vast meadows with lovers eyeing one another from behind Iranian maples, or dancing in loud-voiced ranks beneath the snowcaps.

Their parents—like mine—had been weaned on woozy colonial verses about "pale hands I loved beside the Shalimar" and stories that mingled Persian fables with tales of a "Splendorous Valley." Even my father's not so cheery college classmate, V. S. Naipaul, had evoked a tantalizing vision of a private heaven while describing his weeks on a houseboat on Kashmir's Dal Lake, spiced tea and curried vegetables brought to him as he composed fresh sentences to the sound of kingfishers and the plash of oars.

The same season I traveled across Iran, watching so many chafe against the strictures of an Islamic republic, I knew I had to go to Kashmir, where many were agitating in the opposite direction, towards Islamic rule—or self-determination, at the very least. Now, as I stepped into a green wooden mosque, of the kind found only in this region, I was confronted by papier-mâché walls not to be seen anywhere else in the world. Men sprawled out in the summer heat, while a few pious souls in skullcaps knelt on the carpet, hands raised to Allah.

All around the dusty alleyways of Old Srinagar, white-bearded elders were hobbling along on canes towards the house of prayer, while fair-skinned girls with the green eyes of Afghanistan smiled and sparkled under shawls of orange and yellow and blue. Copper workers in unlit stalls were hammering out beautiful engraved samovars, crafts-people were stitching gold and silver tilla embroidery into elegant shawls. I was wandering through what might have been a series of old canvases here in the bracing mountain air—fifty-one hundred feet above the sea—and much of the snarling congestion and honking fury of the plains seemed very far below.

It was Ramadan now, so the whole green valley was even more on edge than usual. Too hot in the blazing afternoons to work, too early to eat. When I stepped into the central mosque, held up by 378 deodar-wood columns reaching all the way to the roof, it was to see a man with Chinese features under his skullcap meandering past a surge of fountains while, nearby, women gathered on lawns in a happy explosion of bright colors. Then, from every direction—a hundred mosques, so it seemed—the call to prayer rose up and encircled us all, evoking God and the heavens and the need to remember them all; as men streamed in through a little wooden gate, I caught a glimpse, behind them, of bright sunlight, deserted shops, framed visions of green and gold.

For a visitor at least, the presences of 1394, when the mosque was constructed, were overwhelming. The smell of cedarwood was everywhere, and along the Jhelum River, which winds through the center of town, was a jumble of old Hindu temples, crumbling two-story wooden houses, mosques with pagoda towers, next to tidy cottages that might have been set beside the Thames. The closely packed bricks used to construct many of the houses were so intricate and small, I could have been walking through a stage set. "In this medieval town," I remembered reading in Naipaul, "the people were surrounded by wonders."

I made my way along the Bund, the riverside walkway where memsahibs had sauntered even in my parents' youth; finding they were not permitted to buy houses on land, the British began fashioning their own private vision of paradise on the water. Houseboats came up across Dal and Nageen Lakes, re-creating the drawing rooms of Kent, heavy with antimacassars and Grandmother's oak-solid furniture. A home in the colonies allowed them to remake themselves and to take on airs they'd never have gotten away with among neighbors who could read them; here, they could dream up a version of home that had never begun to exist in the country they'd left behind. Even now, much of India has this feeling of a fictional, dressed-up England created by displaced Brits glad to be far from the land they knew. A local Jeeves can solve every one of Bertie's problems in a tropical afternoon.

For centuries, in fact, Kashmir had seemed an answer to many of the world's divisions. It was from here that the ecumenical emperor Ashoka, three hundred years before the death of Christ, had sent Buddhist teachers across Asia to pass on the value of seeing the interdependence of every living thing. It was here, in the sixteenth century, that the emperor Akbar had claimed his "private garden," the area's 777 flowering jewel boxes suggesting the more enduring beauties that await the blessed in heaven. Every summer, huge convoys trundled up from Delhi, four hundred miles away, bearing the emperor, his court, many of Delhi's merchants and at least one hundred thousand horsemen and thirty thousand porters, to what had long been seen as an arboretum for the gods. Even now, the four great gardens around Srinagar—not least Shalimar, its name appearing on perfume bottles and a Royal Navy ship—were gentle places for boys to sit under three-hundred-year-old syca- mores while excited visitors from Ahmadabad or Delhi got themselves up in seventeenth-century Kashmiri costumes for photographs.

"The genius of picnic seems to rule the whole shore of the Dal," a nineteenth-century British journalist had ob- served, and the people from damp England all around him lost their hearts, much as the Moguls had done, to the irises and lupines and wild roses across Kashmir in the spring, the purple saffron fields in September. Local merchants grew famous for spinning magic carpets and jewels tai- lored to a visitor's dreams and when I was at college, Dal Lake became one of those storied rest stops along the mod- ern Silk Road, sung of by Led Zeppelin and associated with the Magic Bus.

You could stay on a houseboat for a fistful of dollars every day (two meals included); the woman across the lake sold honey in saffron and almond and apple flavors (and, if you knew how to ask, spiced with marijuana and opium, too). You could forget the passage of time on floating hotels whose names preserved a grandfather's dream: *Duke of Windsor, Queen Elizabeth, St. James Palace* and even *The Best Prince of Vale.*

A Tibetan prince in the sixteenth century had written to his father (who lived, the son thought, in an earthly paradise

59

called "Shambala"), to evoke Kashmir as a land with "more than three million towns, all filled with houses made of jewels, surrounded by walls of crystal." Its shops sold "emeralds and rubies," he wrote; among its streets filled with singing citizens, "beautiful women with dark blue eyes and lovely figures send you seductive glances."

One day, driving along lanes of poplars as the late light slanted down through the trees, I recalled how even Shah Jahan, cherished for his creation of the Taj Mahal, had constructed a black marble pavilion here, in the Shalimar Gardens, on which was inscribed, in Persian, "If there be a Paradise on earth, it is this, it is this."

———

Kashmir was certainly the paradise that shone inside my mother's heart, at least until she discovered Oxford. Now that she'd turned eighty, I'd begun taking her out every Sunday night to dinner in the Sojourner coffeehouse in Santa Barbara, and as we nibbled on lentil curries or quinoa, she threw open wide the magic doors of her girlhood. The neighbors who eloped and then, tragically, committed themselves to a double-suicide pact. The people down one floor on Marine Drive whose parrots used to devour chilis. The great summer get-togethers on the rambling lawns of the house in Jabalpur. "Nandini, stop that, won't you?" her mild-mannered mother had shouted, not knowing that it wasn't her little daughter who was playing with her toes, but a gate-crashing monkey.

The most lyrical of these tales, though, came from Kashmir, the three trips the family had taken to escape the heat of summer. "Pahalgam," the name of the hill town leading to the mountains, was the open sesame for this treasure chest of memories. "All of us, a big group, went to camp there, for three weeks in August. In the hills. We had porters and cooks so it was very comfortable. I made friends with three wild dogs. I called them Pee-wee and Kiwi and . . . I can't remember now, maybe it was Tee-wee."

On one such trip, the whole party mounted ponies for a five-day trek to the holy Hindu cave at Amarnath. They weren't especially religious, but this was an adventure, the closest you could come in India to Europe. Her elder sister commandeered a sedan chair, but my mother went by pony. In summer, it was said, the ice formations in the Himalayan cave resembled a Shiva lingam.

Soon, however, it began to snow and my mother and her pony got lost. The snow turned into a blizzard, drawing a heavy veil over what had been a cloudless afternoon. The precipice was deep, and the ledge was narrow; her own mother thought she might have lost her youngest daughter forever.

But somehow girl and pony emerged intact—a happy

ending—and Kashmir remained a sanctuary of radiance and calm in my mother's stories, gilded by the seven decades that had passed.

"How old were you?"

"I must have been ten then."

This was 1941, in short, and much of the world was divided by war. Very soon, Japanese soldiers would be pushing across Asia, ever closer to my mother's home.

But Kashmir, during World War II, was a place of peace for my mother—only to be violently parceled off six years later during Partition and turned, while war was subsiding elsewhere, into a place of violence. A parable, almost, about the way Paradise becomes something different in every neighbor's head, and my enchanted garden can never be yours.

The area had always been too seductive for its own good. In the nineteenth century alone, having survived both Mongols and Moguls, it was ruled by Afghans and then by Sikhs, neither of them notably gentle towards Kashmiris; when the British were offered the valley after the Anglo-Sikh War, in 1846, they sold it to a maharajah for a few million rupees and an annual payment of three pairs of Kashmiri shawls and a horse. The rulers of Empire knew that a friendly non-Muslim ruler could prove useful in containing a predominantly Muslim population.

When India claimed independence at last in 1947, the largest of its more than five hundred princely states again seemed doomed to suffer the consequences of geography: two thousand Pashtun militiamen from Pakistan rode into the region, as if to claim it, and the ruling maharajah called on New Delhi for help. India sent its troops up to resist the invaders and, all these decades on, they'd yet to leave. In 1949 the UN suggested that a plebiscite be held so that Kashmiris could themselves decide whether their state remain in largely Hindu India or become part of mostly Muslim Pakistan. Or, best of all, simply rule itself: in 1947 Kashmir had enjoyed its own constitution and flag, its own president and prime minister. But for more than seven decades now, the vote had been constantly talked about and never held. Kashmir became a shorthand for the contention that festers between neighbors whom Empire has cynically divided, as if to cement their differences forever.

Islam had first gained prominence here, I found out, through—of all things—a Tibetan princeling in the fourteenth century, who had been converted by a Sufi preacher; no surprise, perhaps, that many of Srinagar's wooden mosques had pagoda-worthy towers at the top, as if Himalayan Buddhists were building Sunni shrines with the help of designers from Isfahan. Kashmir's location had brought artists here, in the fifteenth century, from Egypt and Turkey and Persia; nowadays, that meant, less happily, that it was bordered by China and Afghanistan and, effectively, Tibet. The only majority Muslim state in largely Hindu India, it was home to twelve million souls who felt surrounded by enemies, whether they were Muslim or Hindu.

Some locals believed that Jesus had been buried in Srinagar, in an area known as "Roza Bal." Others reminded me that five thousand Buddhists had convened here, long before the birth of Christ, to discuss how needless suffering could be transformed. Some even claimed that the Garden of Eden was located in Kashmir, though I couldn't help but wonder whether its abundant apple orchards might evoke the Tree of the Knowledge of Good and Evil even more than the less divisive Tree of Life.

———

In the old city of Srinagar, I found myself in the thick of a conundrum: all the jostle and exoticism of an ancient place that looked unchanged for centuries, surrounded by the checkpoints, the barbed wire, the armed patrols of a never-ending modern conflict. Yet as soon as I drifted onto one of the lakes at the heart of town, suddenly, almost treacherously, all noise fell away, and I was in a forgetful world in which even a trip to a grocery store involved a languorous paddle past lily ponds to a house built on stilts above the reeds.

The first time I stepped into a shikara, or Kashmiri gondola, I wobbled into the boat, lay back on some plush red cushions and, within seconds, as the boatman pushed off, the clamor and dirt of the modern streets, all its congestion, disappeared. Some genie might have waved a wand to make reality dissolve. Even the locals could not resist the spell. "For me," said Malik Nisar, a young Srinagar character who had appointed himself to be my guide, "it's such a stress beater to come out onto the water. When I was growing up, we used to bunk school for a whole day and come out onto the lake. We would hire a boat and go inside, down the backwaters. Just one hour, two hours, and we'd feel better."

A man sat patiently dipping his fishing rod into a lily pond. A woman was picking with furious expertise at lotus roots to mix with her mutton for dinner. Other boats bumped against our shikara, the men at their prows selling saffron, memory cards and what turned out, under a rich purple cloth, to be precious gems. *"Ça va?"* tried one sharp-faced boy, registering my French friend Brigitte, with her camera, next to me one day. "Yesterday, you said today."

He handed her a hugely flowering lotus flower, free of charge. *"Trejoli,"* he announced in a French the Académie française might not have recognized. "*Un cadeau pour maman.*" On his boat was written *Mr. Wonderful*, a title he'd apparently inherited (as quite a few others seemed to have done) from his father, as celebrated a figure on the lake as Mr. Delicious. Centuries of visitors had been won over and exasperated by the resourcefulness of Kashmiri merchants.

Next day, we awoke at 5:00, to see ghostly outlines floating across the water as the sky turned blue-gray. Golden lights shone on the emptiness in front of us. Pictures of four ayatollahs glared down from a shop run by a Shia devotee. And suddenly, amid the chirping of early birds, we came out into an open space and a babble of human voices, as sixty or seventy boats banged against one another, in an aqueous version of dodgems, men in skullcaps chitter-chattering, others gliding around with chilis and onions, whole bags of carrots, one of the merchants pulling out a rusty pair of scales and a rock to measure against some lentils.

For years now, the vegetable market had been luring salesmen who made deals early before heading back to the city and its stalls for a speedy markup; by 7:30 or so, the trading was done, and we were drifting home again as a boat came alongside ours and a boy struck up the ageless cry: "Don't worry. No disturb. Only I am talking. No business. I come from village, and this box—Omar Khayyam—very groovy . . ."

Sometimes the beauty of Kashmir brought me close to tears. There were none of the overhanging clouds, the dingy tower blocks, the broken glass that I'd seen around Kashmir Road and Jerusalem Street in Belfast; for all the bunkers and military camps that encircled us in Srinagar, it was never hard to glimpse the romantic dreams that Bollywood still confected around India's version of a never-never land.

Yet for those born to the enchanted valley, what was most visible was everything that was missing: the four thousand souls, maybe more, who had been unceremoniously "disappeared," the Martyrs' Graveyards housing the thousands who had not. The Palace of Fairies, converted into a vast paramilitary camp; the shrine of the local patron saint of Sufism that, after heavy fighting, was now just rubble. In the lulling silence of the lake, I thought of Salman Rushdie's agonized question about the land of his forebears: was happiness God's gift or the Devil's? He'd begun his book on Kashmir by quoting the local poet Agha Shahid Ali: "I am being rowed through Paradise on a river of hell."

One evening, on the porch of the houseboat he'd owned now for thirty-three years, M. Yousuf Chapri urged me up into the mountains. For sixty-seven of his seventy-three years, the old man had been climbing towards the gods

THE HALF KNOWN LIFE

himself, with Tenzing Norgay, one of the first two men to stand on the summit of Everest, and, in another season, with a postmaster general of the U.S., who'd procured for him the autograph of the first man to set foot on the moon. He'd even named his houseboat *Neil Armstrong*, in honor of man's capacity for scaling the heavens. It was only one year earlier that his son, with a keener nose for what modern visitors crave, had decided to rename it *Sukoon*, in honor of a Sufi word for inner peace.

So Brigitte and I headed out, along with our Kashmir-wise friend Jonny, towards the peaks that have often been seen as an entryway to something higher. We passed walnut trees and mulberries, apricot trees and acacias; on one side of the road marijuana grew as high as my shoulders, and on the other Kashmir's famous cricket bats sat in stacks, like wooden bales, waiting to be claimed by eager Indian tourists. The weather in Kashmir was still as notoriously hard to anticipate as its politics; I'd heard thunder behind the mountains when I awoke, and, within minutes, torrential rains had turned city roads into brown rivers. Half an hour later, we were in brilliant sunshine again, and the song of fresh streams gurgled past us, wooden houses perched here and there peeking out from among the pines.

Pahalgam itself, the center of my mother's fond memories, was now mostly a site for Hindu pilgrims coming by the million to the holy cave at Amarnath; a crush of cheap guesthouses, restaurants advertising vegetarian specialties from every corner of India, worn signs offering "Dandies Carried by 6 Person to Holy Cave and Back." Some fast-track devotees even zipped up to the holy site in helicopters.

We bumped in another direction for seven miles along a rocky path, and then pulled up at last at Aru, where Mr. Chapri's forward-looking son had set up eight blue tents in a meadow, appointed with Kashmiri carpets and high-tech, six-bulbed rectangular flashlights. Two boys rode past on ponies. We wandered up into the hills and past a tall, shawled girl from the nomadic Himalayan Gujar tribe, swishing at her goats. Even higher, in a clearing, were the stone huts where the Gujars lived eighty-five hundred feet above sea level, seemingly untroubled by modernity. I might have been in the very meadow where my mother met her wild dogs, more than seventy years before.

As a few lights came on far below, and stars poked through the clouds above the piney slopes on all four sides, we walked down again and someone served up trout and a whole basket made of caramel while someone else built a campfire. A musician from the local village showed up and sat among us, while a friend used the top of a water jug as a makeshift hand drum, and sang Sufi songs about the taste of wine that is a foretaste of some more heavenly elixir. All night long, I heard the soft breath and clatter of ponies near our tents, the sound of running water; in the morning, washing ourselves in buckets, a chilly baptism, we could see horses trailing down from the mountains.

———

In Kashmir, more than anywhere I'd visited, hope and history were in hourly collision. The area had opened up to visitors like me in the belief that prosperity might sweeten the prospects of those who'd suffered so long through a deadlocked stalemate; yet to come here as a foreigner was to be complicit in the denial of a resolution. Everywhere, I met battered souls wondering how much they could afford to put the sorrows of the past behind them.

One lazy afternoon, Jonny took Brigitte and me to meet an old friend of his who was one of the leading houseboat owners of Kashmir. As we sat on the expansive lawn in the middle of his driveway, Ghulam Butt handed around sandwiches, their crusts tidily cut off, and made it easy for us to imagine ourselves back in the romantic quiet off which his family had lived for generations.

George Harrison had once given a concert on this very lawn, the old man said, along with Ravi Shankar; the grandchildren of Lord Mountbatten had stayed on one of his father's houseboats, for day after slow-moving day. V. S. Naipaul, too. "These last three years have been better," he went on, and I was touched by his eagerness to give us what we wanted; once, he confessed, there had been a siege at Hazratbal Mosque nearby, and the army had seized his property for a month and denied him entry to his own garden.

But this was a time of fresh possibility: Britain and Germany and Japan had all just lifted their travel advisories warning against visits to the area; thirty-six planes now were landing every day. And I guessed that Mr. Butt was trying to fortify himself as well, even as he was extending such courtesy towards us. We represented the possibility of a better future. As we left, though, Jonny extended his condolences and I remembered: only four days earlier, the gracious old man had lost his wife of sixty-three years.

When our SUV pulled out of his driveway, we could see him through the rear window, standing statue-straight, and offering us a crisp military salute as we departed.

For so many around the courtly gentleman, of course, the very notion of a tourist revival when so much remained unresolved was an obscenity. In one place along the Jhelum River, I'd seen the words, scrawled in black letters that nobody could miss, GAZA. Not far away, AL-JIHAD. Even WELCOME TALIBAN. Among the houseboats that traditionally revel in tea-cozy names invoking the British royal family, one was now called *Iraq*, and another, as if in response, *Texas*. Paradise could seem the cruelest notion of all if it meant pretending that the real world didn't exist.

I was determined to see the place called "Jesus's Tomb,"

so I dodged traffic at the center of town later that afternoon and headed down a narrow backstreet. Before I knew it, a young tough was standing in my way. Seconds later, men began appearing from every direction, on foot, on scooters, waving me away. The boy in front of me pulled out a cell phone. Some of his comrades began shouting, grabbing at a camera. How dare anyone suggest a Muslim shrine might have Christian associations?

Back on the houseboat that evening, sipping watermelon-and-ginger juice, I found it hard to imagine Kalashnikovs in the apple orchards, the fighting that would break out a week later. Sometimes, in the Lethean quiet, I thought of the phrase of the fifth-century monk John Cassian: *pax perniciosa*—or the peace that's pernicious because it involves turning your back on the world.

————

One evening, I invited a young Kashmiri to dinner at the stylish new hotel that had come up on Kralsangri Hill, overlooking the lake. His pain had been intensified by the two years he'd spent writing about it at Berkeley, and as we spoke, his voice grew ever louder at the candlelit table under the dark-blue sky.

"Indians walk through our graveyards as if they were gardens," he all but shouted. The very notion of a garden was an insult. "The political problem," he went on, "is that Indians do not accept it's a political problem unless they face a crisis situation. For them it's a law-and-order problem." There were six hundred thousand soldiers in the valley and their presence did more to unsettle the peace than to keep it.

"We're just fighting for a dignified existence," he went on, and his passion was so fierce now that other diners began to look around as lights came on across the water below. "As a free people. Peace without justice is no peace at all."

Only seven years earlier, a "Peace Bridge" had been erected, and a bus permitted—at last—to pass across the "Line of Control" that separates the feuding sides. "'Historic' and 'hope' became much used words," the Kashmiri writer Basharat Peer would report. But after more than sixty years of mortar attacks and suicide bombs, self-determination was no closer than it had ever been.

"In my college days, it was fantastic here," the younger Chapri told me next morning. "But then the guerrillas began going across the border to train, many of them highly educated boys." All but overnight, in August 1989, Chapri, like many, had had to flee. "I had to stop my last year at college. I just took a train down to Delhi with my brother. We had five hundred rupees in our pockets. We knew nobody, we had nowhere to stay." Somehow, they'd managed to find a job, which allowed them to send money back to their parents in Srinagar. Now, after opening two successful boutique properties in southern India, Chapri had decided it was time to bring yoga instructors, Wi-Fi, Thai curries to his embattled hometown.

Jonny was here to encourage that hope, and as our stay drew towards an end, he shared with us his own story. He'd come to the lake first as a very young man, he said, twenty-five years before. He'd brought his girlfriend, Melanie; for all their five years together, she'd been longing to join him on one of his adventures. They'd taken over a room on the *Dream Palace* houseboat and spent fourteen days paddling around the lakes, breathing in the sweet clarity of what could feel like their very own heaven.

Late one evening, however, back in their room, Melanie began to have trouble breathing. Before Jonny knew it, she was in a coma. Next morning, for all his efforts, she was gone, at twenty-four. The victim, it was said, of an asthma attack.

"Kashmir changed my life," said Jonny. "It continues to change my life. I mean, suddenly I was in this Kashmiri world of hospitals and police stations and the mortuary and burial rites. Everything you never want or expect to see. And there'd been a report in the paper that a foreign woman had died under mysterious circumstances. So I was taken to be questioned by the police. For twelve hours."

He'd had to call Melanie's parents back in England to tell them that their girl was dead. He'd had to make contact with a consulate, to arrange for Melanie's body to be taken back home. "It still hits me emotionally," he went on, to walk the streets he'd had to walk through for six agonized days as he went from one sorrow to the next. I realized, too late, what it must have cost him when I asked if we could pass through a small green door at the center of town that led to the Christian cemetery, which must have brought back to him the death that had touched him so directly.

Such a tragedy could have cut the life of any young traveler in two. But Jonny, remarkably, decided he wouldn't turn his back on Kashmir; he set up a tour company and became the first foreigner to lead trekkers around the valley. Only weeks before we arrived, he'd actually arranged for a room for his twenty-one-year-old niece on the very *Dream Palace* houseboat where he'd suffered his loss. The place that had threatened to take away his heart would be the one where he remade it, and—he sincerely hoped—did his small part to remake Kashmir's broken heart as well.

So what should I tell my eighty-two-year-old mother when I got home? Could her memories of Kashmir still be found? Should they? The very British who had raised her and educated her so beautifully had also cut the honeymooners' valley into pieces and left it in the hands of implacable rivals; tourists were coming back now, her son among them, but in the face of a reality of roadblocks and regular confrontations.

From the sundeck of the houseboat named for inner peace, I watched four schoolgirls in spotless white salwar kameez, white shawls around their heart-shaped faces, paddle through the quiet of the morning; a man in a nearby skiff was offering to heat up fresh fish and chicken in a tumble of hot coals in his boat. The previous night, a musician had stepped onto our houseboat and, seated against silk pillows, flanked by hurricane lights, played a hundred-string santour: another Sufi melody about the soul's crying out for home, a place where no divisions exist.

In Varanasi, pilgrims come to bathe in the filthy waters, and barely descry, through the mist, a thin sandbank that seems to represent the other shore. Here, among the egrets and lotus ponds, I seemed at times to have arrived on that other shore, looking back on the real world. In the slumberous quiet of the lake, it was hard to tell Hindu from Muslim; "conflict" seemed a word in a foreign language. All I could catch were the bright colors of the "7-D Entertainment Center" across the water, offering fresh tourist delights. The nearby houseboat, *Give-N-Take*, advertising kahwa, a soothing Kashmiri almond and saffron and cinnamon tea. The cries in the distance of children, as they clambered into a helium balloon at the funfair to rise to its "VIP" height of 350 feet, every last one of their tickets bearing the legend "Break Down Fear / Relief Is Here."

Wrath

M y college classmate Nicolas—the most fascinating
friend I made in my student years, not least because
he was the hardest to anticipate—would have felt entirely
at home in Kashmir; he always seemed to find his way
to places where the possibility of transcendence rubbed
against the less exalted facts of life. For many years, in fact,
he'd been living as a war correspondent, spending months
on end in the Hotel Palestine in Baghdad, in San Salvador,
in Kosovo and anywhere where there was strife. Yet every
time he emerged from these conflicts, he flew back to the
Australian interior—the red-dirt emptiness at the heart of
the oldest continent—and started to take long drives out
towards horizons that, for all the oblivion they threatened,
promised liberation from the complications of both self
and history.

When first we met, we were teenagers, and Nicolas was

already a legendary scholar of Homer and Virgil. Incurious in youth, my friends and I never bothered to learn where he came from, though there were rumors of a mother in Prague, a boyhood in Paris, Swiss boarding schools; only much later did I learn that the English that he spoke with such demolishing fluency was in fact his fourth or maybe fifth language, mastered when he came to a medieval English high school at the age of twelve. All we knew was that we almost never saw him in the daylight and he always dressed in black.

It was usually close to midnight when I made the long trek up three flights of stairs to his room at the top of the New Building, constructed in 1733. The curtains were always drawn, and there were generally a couple of figures stretched out on sofas or ingesting something in one corner. When the door opened, I'd see a rail-thin figure, very tall, with a monk's black tonsure above his very pale face; he let me in with negligent courtesy, and soon he'd be delivering exquisite sentences on folly and vanity and much else that could dazzle an eighteen-year-old.

Copies of *Against Nature* and *Les Fleurs du Mal* lay on tables, under the shaded lamps; a blonde in an all-black catsuit appeared now and then before vanishing again into the night. Nicolas didn't seem young—or old—and part of his charisma came from the fact we couldn't begin to place him in any way. He was the youngest among us in years, and he took his final exams twelve months early; he dashed off the essays for those exams in a hand so fast and illegible that he had to be summoned back from London, to which he'd decamped long before, to come and read every word aloud.

Many of us, in truth, feared for him, because it was hard to imagine a place for such a soul in a world that was not always so sensitive or refined. Seven years after we left college, there was a knock on my door in my studio apartment in New York, close to midnight, and it was Nicolas, without explanation, accompanied by a rock star's girlfriend. I pressed the twenty dollars he needed into his hand and he disappeared towards some dark corner on the Lower East Side.

Twenty years after that, I found myself one summer day in Perth and a new friend asked if I happened to know this somewhat mythical figure, who seemed to be my age and had been at the college named for Mary Magdalene at the same time as I. He was writing books now, she said, and when I picked up one of his works, I found him sharing vivid, funny, often terrifying accounts of his drives deep into the enveloping vacancy of the interior, as if to work through the war-bombed Europe of his boyhood and come out on the other side.

He was living with an Aboriginal woman, I heard, always in remote places, and he had steeped himself in indigenous lore, though remaining punctilious about never giving away any of its secrets or presuming to know more than he did. As I read deeper, I saw something in the haunted, humble works that I could not turn away from. Nicolas had the intelligence to see that no rebirth is possible without a painful extinction. He also showed me, in his prose, how the traditional owners of Australia were fascinated by the holy lands of the Middle East.

Whenever he was traveling amid the charged spaces of the Sinai, he wrote, he tried to see them through the marveling eyes of Aboriginal friends; they could never hear enough about the Christian deserts. They loved to learn about the wilderness where the "evil one" had tried to tempt the Savior, the Outback of the Old Testament. The first whitefellas they'd met, in many cases, were missionaries from northern Europe, and the traditional people respected anyone who had a sense of powers beyond human reckoning. Most Aboriginal souls, in fact, now identified themselves as Christian, though without ever relinquishing the subtle and complex theology they had inherited along with the land seeded by creator spirits and rich with sacred sites.

Once, Nicolas wrote, he was walking through Jerusalem, trying to clear his head of memories of war, and he found his way to the Russian Church of Mary Magdalene above Gethsemane. A young nun was praying there—she offered to pray for him, too—and she lit up when she learned that he lived among the brush fires and cyclones of inner Australia. From her cell she brought back the picture she kept there, of, improbably, an Aboriginal landscape, called *The Promised Land*.

I couldn't track down my old friend while I was in Perth, but, quickened by what I'd read in his eerie and unforgettable books—the first was called *Heaven and Earth*—I chose the remotest town I could find, a speck on the map fourteen hundred miles from Perth, itself self-described as the "loneliest regional capital in the world," and flew up there. For two and a half hours the plane passed over red-brown lizard-skin that might have been the Grand Canyon laid on its side. From the air, it looked uncannily like an Aboriginal dot painting.

When I touched down in Broome—all corrugated-iron huts and slowly turning fans—I dropped off my bags and began looking around the few empty streets at its center. In front of an outdoors movie house, the Sun Picture Gardens, was a little sign. I leaned in to read more about what was said to be the oldest such establishment on the planet.

As I was transcribing the details, I heard a shout, very close. "Who are you?"

I looked around. An Aboriginal man, no more than three feet away, was staring at me with undisguised rage.

"What are you doing here?"

I fumbled out some kind of answer—"Just looking"—but he wasn't satisfied. I began walking down the street, away from him, but he kept reeling beside me, his anger rising to a pitch.

I picked up speed, but I could no more get rid of him than of my shadow. He was right, I knew: I didn't belong here. And he did. But now the tourist shops and pearl galleries lined up along the empty streets had consigned him and his relatives to a patch of grass on the edge of town.

I'd already seen other Aboriginal people trooping along the straight roads out of town, heads to the ground, retracing, a romantic might say, the secret paths of their ancestors. Occasional Outlanders whooshed past, as if from some parallel reality. The locals all around me seemed as foreign to the world I knew as the elements throwing up dramas in the heavens might.

Desperate now to put some distance between myself and the traditional owner, I started walking faster, in the direction of the tourist information center, not many blocks away. Outside its entrance stood two overturned shopping carts. Assembled on the grass, a cluster of Aboriginal men.

"Where's your umbrella then?" one of them called out.

Was he mocking me for my urban cluelessness—or actually predicting rain? It hardly mattered. I'd come here in the middle of summer, when 110-degree-Fahrenheit days leave the streets desolate and punishing, and now I was in the thick of the "buildup," the annual rumblings of thunder that signal the coming of torrential downpours.

I saw a taxi and jumped in, asking to be taken to the famous wide, golden beach on the other side of town that leads towards a beach that stretches for one hundred and forty miles.

When I got out, not a soul was to be seen. It was 3:30 in the afternoon in Broome, and everything—even the public restroom—was shuttered for the day.

———

Seventeen years earlier, I'd flown over to Australia to spend weeks crisscrossing the continent of new futures in honor of its bicentenary year. I'd driven up the east coast all the way to Surfers Paradise, its attractions tricked up in Japanese signs and pricings in yen to lure the dominant travelers of the time. I'd explored the Great Barrier Reef and wandered around the drizzly penal institutions of Tasmania. I'd spent days in Melbourne and Canberra and Adelaide, and even taken a train said to follow the tracks of the Afghan camel drivers of the nineteenth century, all the way to Alice Springs.

But only one place remained with me for years after I left, in part because it fit inside no pigeonhole in my head.

Uluru—"Ayers Rock," as it was still called then—exerted an almost unnerving magnetism. I had sensed its presence before I saw it, and it stayed with me long after I departed. Even I, an outsider, could feel the spirits of creator beings within the eleven-hundred-foot-tall "island mountain," the millennia-old stories of willie wagtails and feuding serpents that intersected here, two hundred miles from the nearest small town.

In urban Australia I'd surrendered to the traveler's easy assumption that I was surrounded by the dry ironies of Britain amid the sunny ease of a barefoot, easygoing California; here, I told myself, was a society of cheerfully disenchanted renegades set down in Laguna Beach. But the interior made such glibness feel very small indeed; the red rocks and canyons might remind me of Arizona and Utah, but they breathed with an intensity, a sense of the ancient, that I'd found in no natural landscape before.

I couldn't say it was paradise but, more, a different kind of reality; and what gave it its fascination was that the traditional owners had never lost contact with their gods. Faithfully, they kept linking heaven and earth with their songs, while the rest of us remained stranded in perplexity, able to feel the power of the rocks, but not to read any of their runes. Inner Australia lived in a language few of us could speak.

Now, as I looked out from my tiny motel room, electrical storms were breaking across the bay. Nighttime clouds were illuminated by long, silent flashes, as if the heavens themselves were submitting to an X-ray. Again and again, again. I opened the door and saw mangrove trees shuddering in a furious wind. I slammed it shut again because the red-dirt earth all round seemed to be thrumming with such intensity that I could imagine it on the move towards me.

The features of Broome didn't make sense to me; the place was celebrated for the "horizontal waterfalls" a relatively short drive away; not long before, it had seen nineteen inches of rain in a single day. Crocodiles here could trace back their ancestry 250 million years; Roebuck Bay, just outside my window, was said to be the only place on the continent where dinosaur tracks were woven into the sacred geography sung into being by wandering ancestors. I thought of how D. H. Lawrence had felt "unborn" in the "pre-world" of Australia. "Strange old feelings wake in the soul," he had written, evoking "the utter loneliness, the manlessness, the untouched blue sky overhead, the gaunt, lightless gum-trees rearing a little way off."

Shortly before 1883, the largest species of pearl oyster ever to have been found was discovered just off the coast near Broome. Within a generation, the dot on Australia's empty northern coast was in command of eighty percent of the world's pearl trade. Less often emphasized was the fact that the business was in many cases the plaything of adventurers and escaped convicts; hundreds of indigenous people were found beaten, murdered or simply cast off in remote places once their services were no longer of use.

Even now, the city dwellers I met here had clearly come to live in societies of one, at sharp angles to life as most of us know it. The cabbie who picked me up after dark one night was a husky-voiced matron who told me that she cleaned her car every day at 3:00 a.m. "Haven't worn a pair of long pants in three years," the driver of the town bus shouted back to me after offering a fair reading of the day's tides. "Don't even own a pair of long pants anymore." There was no mail delivery to residences in Broome, as if to suggest that nobody was at home.

In the window of the local bookshop gleamed an ad for a medium workshop led by a "clairvoyant spiritual counsellor who works with light-beings from the Angelic, Elemental and Multi-Dimensional realms." Encircled by traditional elders whose elemental realms were many degrees more multi-dimensional, the ad could only look a little poignant. The Aboriginal people might call themselves Christian, but they did not understand why Europeans needed to go into a special house to talk to God, eyes closed. For them, the promised land was nowhere but the land around them.

Visitors get lost in Broome, I heard, or lose a grip on themselves. When I returned to the tourist information center, past the overturned shopping carts and the taunts of the locals, I found the noticeboards full of warnings, and news of roads closed for the next three months. At some point, in fact, I realized that I was moving, in Broome, through a jungle of terrified alerts. This is what to do if you are stung by a box jellyfish, said the signs at Cable Beach. "Ants are a problem in tropical conditions," offered the notice by the tea-making machine in my motel room. The reception desk closed down at 9:30 p.m., advising guests to contact the Broome police if something came up after dark.

I was in a kind of holy land, I thought, not so different from the vibrant, chastened sense of the heavens and their whims I'd met in Shakespeare or Homer. I could understand why my friend, intimate with Latin and Greek texts and their sense of fates determining our destinies, had settled here; I sensed an Old Testament humility and attentiveness all around, as the traditional people set their own fires to contain the flames of heaven and made their peace with tsunamis and up to twenty cyclones a year. When I went, years later, to a place serving kangaroo tacos in Alice Springs, I glimpsed on the arm of the fresh-faced, friendly college-age kid who handed them over to me a tattoo of the first word of *The Iliad*: μῆνιν, or "wrath."

One morning, when I awoke, a shrill wind was blowing through the settlement, as if to underline how provisional such communities remain. Everything seemed to be in motion here, as if the Aboriginal people's wanderings—across what for them was a kind of scripture—had been passed down to the rest of us, though without the understanding or the sense of divinity. In the winter months, the moon creates an uncanny effect on the nearby ocean that resembles a golden staircase.

Sometimes there were winds of ninety-five miles an hour here, I heard, and when I stepped into the town's most elegant establishment for selling pearls, at 10:00 a.m., I noticed that its clock showed 6:30. The common death adder and the desert death adder were everywhere in this desert, and water pythons lay in the middle of the road to the east, at twilight, waiting to devour dusky rats. Australia is said to be the only country where the majority of serpents are venomous.

Irruptions had long been the defining theme of local mythology, I knew; I'd seen it at the cinema in every Aussie movie from *Picnic at Hanging Rock* to *Walkabout*, from *Japanese Story* to *The Last Wave*. Kids get snatched by dingoes. Demure little girls in Victorian frocks step out of their verses from Tennyson and disappear. Beings from another world loom above your bed.

But this was no movie and when I walked out of the local bookshop that afternoon, it was to see black thunderclouds gathering over the ocean, while parts of the sky remained brilliantly cobalt.

I began heading back to my motel along the eerily de-serted roads, as in some upended Sahara. The wind roared in my ears, whistling through the shells of beat-up cars parked—or abandoned—next to homemade shacks along the way. The ocean was a turquoise plate not far away— red-dirt roads here run right into the white sands and blue-green waters—and then my heart began to pound as some figures emerged from their shacks and started walking to-wards me.

It didn't really matter which of us, if either, was in the wrong. This wasn't my place, and it had been theirs for six hundred centuries or more.

I walked faster, and saw more figures all around. I looked straight ahead of me and tried to pretend that, as in other dispossessed parts of the world, my dark skin might offer some kind of protection, even kinship. I started to run. When I got to my little room, I bolted the door behind me and, out of breath, dialed a number I knew by heart.

"What is it?" worried my wife, thousands of miles away, in Japan. "I wasn't expecting you to call."

"I just need the sound of a familiar voice."

Then, outside, the downpour began, like something from a biblical prophecy. A few hours later, electrical storms above the mangrove swamps began offering illuminated flash-pictures of the clouds.

I was in the presence of something immense, I knew,

and nothing I could begin to control or anticipate. This promised land reminded me that I, illiterate here, could remain only an intruder. When I opened my door next morning, just a crack, the wide-open spaces all around seemed thick with energy, alive.

The Holy City

Not many seasons later, in another holy land, I felt myself pulled towards the Ethiopians. They were standing in a quiet corner of the Church of the Holy Sepulchre, up a flight of stairs: just four bearded priests, leaning on their shepherd's crooks, delivering a slow, ancient melody as they intoned from their illuminated copies of the Bible. I had seldom been so moved as when I traveled across Ethiopia one sunny winter, and found the Book of Kings coming to life all around me: in a place of war and famine, faith shone more vividly than almost anywhere, both sustenance and solace. All across the highlands I saw pilgrims, clad in white, carrying almost nothing, walking across the parched open spaces to pay their respects to a holy cave or shrine.

The hushed dignity of their devotion; the way they gathered, carrying candles, in darkened graveyards on their Christmas Eve, to sing hymns around what looked to be a manger; the cross-shaped windows and palm-sized Bibles: it shook me out of words. And here in Jerusalem, the withdrawn solemnity of their Amharic chanting served as an anchor as the rush, the clamor—the fury—of conviction threatened to swallow me up the minute I stepped out into the crowded streets.

I had arrived on a Friday, which meant that the faithful were streaming through the jostled alleyways of the Old City for prayers at the mosque that sits atop Temple Mount, its golden dome a famously contested vision of heaven. And it was only a few days after Christmas, which meant that large groups of Christians, from France and Italy, had gathered along the Via Dolorosa. One pilgrim was shaking under the weight of a huge wooden cross, his friends singing as he bore it down the narrow passageway, and then he broke into sobs as he labored under the burden of re-creating the walk of his Savior, on a very different Friday two thousand years before.

By the time I made it to the Western Wall, not many minutes away, the great open space in front of it was thronged, and there was no space for even a single extra body. Men in black hats were rocking back and forth against the ancient stones, muttering prayers or sticking pieces of paper into its crevices; on the other side of a barrier, younger members of the faith were gathering in large circles, arms around one another's shoulders as they greeted the Sabbath with dance and song.

Where could a nonaffiliated soul take shelter? I began to wonder. How make peace among all the competing chants? I headed back to the Church of the Holy Sepulchre, where many believe Jesus was crucified. A group of Chinese petitioners was paging through the *Ad lapidem unctionis* in Mandarin. Some Russians were bustling into a tiny alcove to kiss a sacred icon. Troops of burly Armenian monks in dark, heavy robes were shaking the old stone walls with their chants, as if determined to drown out the Franciscans in a balcony above, sending up their own candlelit prayers.

I could hear no single clear note for the clamor all around, so I stepped out of the main chapel and returned to the courtyard and climbed the stairs to where the Ethiopians were murmuring almost inaudibly, neglected by the world. This Chapel of St. Michael was, for complex historical reasons, said to belong officially to the Copts. Both groups slept on the rooftop a few steps up, but often they'd come to blows over the tiny territory they shared. On one occasion Israel's Supreme Court had had to settle the bloody dispute; on another, the government in neighboring Jordan had been forced to intercede.

Thus, notoriously, Jerusalem: a riot of views of paradise overlapping at crooked angles till one was left with the sorrow of six different Christian orders sharing the same space, and lashing out at one another with brooms.

————

I'd come to the holy city comfortable in the expectation I'd remain untouched; as someone who was neither Christian nor Muslim nor Jew, I was sure I could observe the rites and worship of every group without recoiling from any. But within hours of my arrival I was catching passion like a fever; it was hard to stand apart from a crowd in a jam-packed passageway, even when I lost all sense of which holy place the masses were pushing me towards.

It had long been too easy to say that Jerusalem is our world in miniature: the family home in which everyone is squabbling with his siblings over a late father's will. Days before my arrival, peace talks had broken out—again—between Israelis and Palestinians. But peacemakers everywhere, from Gandhi's India to Martin Luther King's Atlanta, are irresistible targets for the violent. Some Palestinians began launching rocket attacks from their displaced territories. Israeli soldiers stormed into those areas to try to silence the attacks. The latest American president announced he'd be making his first visit to the Holy Land two days before I planned to go to Bethlehem. Observers got ready to hold forth yet again on what has to happen when an outsider sticks his hand into a hornet's nest.

Yet Jerusalem spoke for a peculiarly twenty-first-century challenge as well, as the dissolution of borders meant that more and more conflicts were internal. In Kashmir, in Belfast, in Tibet, I'd witnessed one belief system up against another; in Jerusalem, the fighting was not just between traditions, but within them. Orthodox Jews were spitting at their secular brothers, while those brothers were pinning posters of Botticelli's *Birth of Venus* on synagogue doors to affront their sensitive coreligionists. Sunni Muslims lived harmoniously together within the country's borders, but they were ringed on every side by Shia, who were pledged to committing Israel to oblivion. Far right often made common cause with far left here—ultra-Orthodox Jew aligning with Palestine Liberation Organization—on the grounds that my enemy's enemy must be my friend.

The Pope himself had, in my lifetime, been denied permission to pray in the Greek chapel of what is often regarded as the holiest site in Christendom, the Church of the Holy Sepulchre. And doubters could always point out that the emperor who had ordered that church's construction, Constantine, had murdered his own wife and son. An English traveler in the nineteenth century who'd gone to observe "Holy Fire"—the apparently miraculous appearance of a light in a crevice in the church on the Saturday of Easter Week, announcing the rebirth of the world—had found himself stepping over "a great heap of bodies" after a stampede in which "soldiers with their bayonets killed a number of fainting wretches, the walls splattered with the blood and brains of men who had been felled like oxen." Skeptics could never get enough of the fact that members of the same religion would start assaulting one another simply because the Greek interpretation of a holy book differed from the Franciscan.

Jerusalem was a parable that had turned into a cautionary tale, a warning about what we do when we're convinced we know it all. A Jonathan loses his temper and every Jew is condemned to perdition; a Salman misspeaks and every Muslim is assaulted. Even those who had worked to turn the place into a long-planned New Jerusalem could not wish away the bloodstains all around. It was Theodor Herzl, the spiritual founder of the Jewish state, who had written, as to the holy city, "The musty deposits of 2,000 years of inhumanity, intolerance and foulness lie in your reeking alleys." It was the first president of Israel, Chaim Weizmann, who had observed of Jerusalem, "Anything done to desecrate and defile the sacred has been done. It's impossible to imagine so much falsehood and blasphemy."

Yet in Jerusalem, more than anywhere, hope remained as stubborn as resentment. It had to: to give up on Jerusa-

lem, after all that it had survived, was to give up on even
the prospect of improving our lot. One morning I strolled
around the Bible Lands Museum in West Jerusalem, a
strikingly elegant collection of mostly Egyptian and Sume-
rian artifacts. A sign there pointed out that the star, though
central to Jewish lore, could also be found in Islam and
Christianity. The dove, a text went on, was as important to
Jewish symbology as to Christian. Even the menorah had
been found carved onto Christian catacombs in Rome, im-
pressed upon Umayyad coins in Damascus.

But no one in Jerusalem expects easy answers soon, or
solutions. Not far from all the ecumenical signs, some wise
soul had seen fit to issue a warning. "Ancient Egyptians seldom entered temples," a sign advised. "Like modern atomic
reactors, they were complex and dangerous sources of power,
requiring special decontamination procedures for the few
people who entered them."

I was back in the red-dirt emptiness of Australia, in a
way, where the traditional owners took pains to erect invisible barbed wire around the sacred, if only to remind us
that men should not meddle with the work of gods. Yet
Jerusalem also remained the place where such warnings
went most vividly unheeded. It made me think of the deeply
thoughtful soul who had overseen the development of the
atom bomb. When he recalled what he'd loosed upon the
world, he'd looked ashen, and quoted from the *Bhagavad*

Gita: "Now I am become Death, the destroyer of worlds."
The "American Prometheus" spent the rest of his life trying
to contain what he had helped to create.

————

Every time I walked through Damascus Gate, however, I
found myself back in something as irreducible as life. Little
boys wove through the crowded alleyways, carrying glasses
of tea on trays above their heads, while older brothers
pushed large carts of supplies down slippery ramps through
the ill-lit souk, one boy standing in front of the descending
vehicle so it wouldn't careen away. Most of the shops in the
Muslim Quarter on a midwinter morning were quiet—save
for some beautiful Koranic chanting from a scratchy radio
in a café. But as soon as midday prayers were over, the area
around the gate swarmed with vendors selling enormous
pink teddy bears, cell phone covers, bras, and hot ears of
corn. There were garbanzo beans on one side, Nokias on
the other.

I might have been in any bazaar in Fez or outside the
Umayyad Mosque in Damascus. But the videos on sale
along the streets here had names like *Ramallah 2*, and the
first sign I saw, on stepping into the Austrian Hospice in
search of some respite from the noise, declared, "The entry
with a weapon is not permitted." The men standing outside

shops like Abraham Antiquities—right next to the Ali Baba Internet Center—were shouting, "Golgotha? That way!" and "India, India, please. I need to talk to you. For two minutes only."

There was a strong smell of cardamom everywhere— then of freshly baked bread and incense—and as I wandered into the Ecce Homo chapel, suddenly the call to prayer rose above me, and I found myself inside an overlapping of chants from mosques on every side. A Coptic priest was hurrying past, his black skullcap with gold crosses suggesting a visitor from another world; Armenian priests with dark hoods over their heads, as if descending from *The Seventh Seal*, were turning from Christian Quarter Road onto David Street. Among all the shops selling postcards, "Guns 'N' Moses" T-shirts, replicas of the true cross, flyers had been plastered reading GOD WON'T RESURRECT THOSE WHO WON'T SAVE HIS CREATION.

A tour guide near the Western Wall was explaining to his flock that the stones over which we were walking were seventeen hundred years old, dating from Roman times; with every step we were treading upon crypts and underground tombs, memories of a time when five hundred Jews were crucified each day, till the Romans ran out of space and wood. I couldn't help remembering that Carl Gustav Jung had once dreamed he was in a ten-story building, and descending deeper and still deeper. When he awoke, he sensed he'd been dreaming of Jerusalem, which for him might have been a visible reflection of the collective unconscious.

Yet what kept astonishing me as I walked among the memories of wars and crusades was not how full of death the place seemed, but how alive. A bar mitzvah was being held in the tunnel leading to the Wall, and most of the figures vaulting past me now wore the long forelocks and high black hats of the Haredim, those "who tremble before God." What deepened the impact was not how much lay underground, but how much was on the surface. Jerusalem is "a burning city," I had read in the pages of its eloquent local son Amos Oz. "But a closer glance reveals an immeasurable weightiness."

Perhaps he meant simply that Jerusalem is a city of fire and earth. Every time I looked down, I saw pistachio shells and refuse and trampled fruit; every time I looked up, I saw a grid of church towers, minarets and (to speak for our modern faith) satellite dishes. This was an unusually rooted place, I began to think, that was always about to go up in flames.

———

I was born in a city partly founded by monks. But Oxford, by the time I entered the world, was a gray and ghostly place, its fires long extinguished. Yes, my little friends and I played "I Spy" games using Christian picture books and sang of "a green hill far away"—Calvary—on damp winter mornings at school. All of us knew that it was just up the street, on the thoroughfare named St. Giles', that the believer from Belfast had dreamed up parables of a talking lion who spoke for Jesus, not many feet from the central Martyrs' Memorial, recalling the three sixteenth-century bishops who had been burned there for their refusal to renounce their Protestant faith.

Yet even as we sang our hymns of affirmation, Empire was coming apart and the country was losing its faith in more or less everything, starting with itself. The philosophers who were my parents' colleagues devoted their energies to "denoting phrases" and niceties of logic; the prayers we recited every morning were turned into singsong incantations as rote as nursery rhymes. We inched through the Gospel of Matthew in the Greek, but only with a view to learning about aorist tenses and irregular verbs; the verses about praying in private, "in the secret place," the reminder that "if your eye is sound, your whole body will be filled with light" were all obscured by grammar.

So how could I not catch fire in Jerusalem? Everything was at stake here. And the lines were so clearly drawn that almost everything constituted a trespass. My first morning in the city, I was told I could not take notes on the Sabbath at the Western Wall. A Greek woman upbraided me in the Church of the Holy Sepulchre for standing with my hands joined behind my back. When I'd tried to walk up to the mosque on Temple Mount, the "Noble Sanctuary," I'd been stopped by guards and told that visitors could no longer enter. Even Muslims, I was reminded, had to answer detailed questions on the Koran before being granted admission.

Nothing was taken for granted here, and everything had significance. This was so unlike what I knew that I quit my comfortable hotel, a safe fifteen-minute walk from Damascus Gate, and walked through that crowded entrance again to post myself in the midst of the conflagration. Around me, as I settled into a room on the Way of Suffering, bells seemed to be tolling through the day; every time I stepped out of the hospice, the smell of sweetmeats made me feel I was inside a ceremonial feast. On all sides, the ageless cries of Jerusalem encircled me, celebrating the mingling of sacred and profane. "Hey, Russka! *Buona sera!* I sell you this for three euros. Three dollars. Hey! This is the six-and-a-half station of the cross!"

The Old City seemed a riot of merchants and pilgrims, each one advancing his own vision of salvation. But even when I went out into modern West Jerusalem, whose shopping malls brought me back into a New World suburb, I had only to turn off a main street, and I was again in a holy turbulence.

One bright afternoon, I found myself, by mistake, in Me'a She'arim, the ultra-Orthodox quarter, where men in the black and white clothes of eighteenth-century Europe were pushing along babies in supermarket carts. Above us, in the displacing streets, signs announced, JEWS ARE NOT ZIONISTS—ZIONISTS ARE NOT JEWS, ONLY RACISTS. WE PRAY TO G-D FOR AN IMMEDIATE END OF ZIONISM AND THEIR OCCUPATION. I was all set to draw conclusions from this when I learned that there were nineteen factions within the ultra-Orthodox community alone, so anything I could say about one person was probably disproved by his neighbor.

I headed back to the Old City and found myself in front of a "Map of the Armenian Genocide"; the museum nearby gave me the decapitated heads and slaughtered children of the savageries of 1915. Minutes later, I was inside the "Chamber of the Holocaust," looking at sacred scrolls that had been defaced and Torahs drenched in blood. A pilgrim, very often, is traveling in search of the past; but Jerusalem was the center of a thousand clashing pasts, and all of them made up the nightmare from which it was longing to awaken. When I traced my way back to the Austrian Hospice that evening, I couldn't rest for all the voices crowding in on me.

Jerusalem, I was coming to think, was the place where everyday morality and religion part ways, on grounds of irreconcilable differences. The scriptures that had come to light here were essentially a training in how inadequate all human logic remains. A prodigal son is feted while his loyal brother is ignored. A lost sheep is worth ninety-nine others who remain safely in the fold. Poor Job proves his devotion to the Lord again and again and is rewarded with ever more baroque punishments. Right and wrong were as beside the point here as cause and effect, if only because heavenly justice is, by definition, impossible for mortals to follow. It was no surprise that Jerusalem had made as many skeptics of believers as it had made believers of skeptics.

Unable to turn my mind off, I got out of bed again and put on my shirt and jeans. I stepped out into the long, silent corridor with its copies of old maps and texts along the walls. I walked up to the rooftop of the hospice. As I stood there in the midwinter dark, looking out at red crosses, the moon, the green lights of minarets, everything seemed blessedly untroubled, a paradise of calm.

From high above, all the dissenting parts made for a kind of whole. Up here, you could forget distinctions between the sects; the narcissism of small differences made little sense at all. I thought of what I had felt on the rooftop of the Church of the Holy Sepulchre: bells are most moving when you don't know where they're coming from.

Then, since it was almost daybreak, I went down again, and out, into the chill alleyways, almost deserted now. A faint light began to show up between the buildings and I almost walked into a large Greek Orthodox priest—thick black robes and heavy beard—leading a group of believers around his sanctuary. Hooded figures, hands pushed into pockets against the cold, were passing under a cobbled archway to attend the day's first prayers at the mosque. In the warm, illuminated cave next to the Western Wall, dozens of Orthodox Jews were already in full chant, banging their heads against the stones and intoning verses from the Torah. One of them, wild-eyed, with flowing ringlets, pushed into my hands a copy of a book on Emunah, the kind of faith that leads to righteousness.

I might have been walking through Jung's diagram of the subconscious, in a city made up only of inner lives, always in full throat. And the question at the heart of every one was as simple as it was unanswerable: how make peace and passion rhyme?

———

Inner Australia had shaken me because it had shown me how threadbare every human settlement—and certainty— must remain; the traditional owners had learned to read the signs of brush fire and flash flood, yet their wisdom seemed to come in the form of knowing how little they could do to control them. Yet here in Jerusalem, humans were so sure of their gods that each one drew, in rough bold strokes, his own image of paradise on top of somebody else's; it was dangerously easy to believe that what we do with heaven is even more important than what heaven does to us.

"Wandering among the tombs," Melville had written, during his eighteen-day trip to the Holy Land—he never quite came back to earth again—"I began to think myself one of the possessed with devils." Everything was broken here, he felt, and stony; he lay awake all night along the coast, listening to the surge of the sea. The city of worship was for him most striking for "cemeteries all around," and after he returned to New York, he barely wrote again.

Melville's words shivered inside me because it was he who had stressed how every scripture must make a place for devils, and how those closest to the holy are often on closest terms with demons. The Desert Fathers hadn't gone into the wilderness just to see the light; they were there to do undistracted battle with the dark. It was Melville who brought into hopeful young America the reminder that Icarus flew too close to the sun; the notion that humans can be stronger than Nature or Fate renders the half known life a devastation.

Yet still, almost in spite of himself, Melville found himself pulled back, again and again—as, now, did I—to the Church of the Holy Sepulchre, the very center of tumult that I'd been so happy to escape my first day here. I started going there at sunset every evening, to stand on the roof encircled by bells and chants as the golden light glanced off the Jerusalem stone. And then I started going there every morning before sunrise, too, as if to prepare for the contention to come.

Every time I entered, I walked past the slab on which Jesus's body was said to have been laid, and hurried by the lines of petitioners waiting to crowd into the innermost sanctum, the tomb. I preferred the other, largely neglected side of the vast space, and made my way to a small barren cave, as it seemed, in which, very often, a single candle had been placed upon a ledge.

There was nothing else there, really, which meant it could be filled with anything at all. The raggedness, the worn irregularity of the space went right through me. The empty hollow looked as broken as everything human, as clear as whatever we deem holy.

I didn't do anything in the unfurnished antechamber other than sit, sometimes with my own thoughts, sometimes watching the world shuffle by. There was nothing to command the senses. I could not have said how much this was a man-made construction, how much a crack in the rocks. One day I heard that this was "Christ's Prison," where Jesus had awaited crucifixion, but then I learned that four other places were also so denominated.

All I knew was that this rough chapel was liberation from chatter and from text.

As I emerged from my sanctuary one bright morning, it was to be reminded of everything I'd been fleeing. "For me, to be honest," a tour guide was saying to his group, outside in the courtyard in the early sunlight, "being here is so foreign. It's not the place but the people who come here who give it truth."

"It's dark," someone else was intoning, "and smelly and full of dirt." One reason, no doubt, why General Gordon (the doomed British hero from the Siege of Khartoum) had devoted many years to "proving" that Constantine's church was not in fact the place where Jesus died. Golgotha, Gordon had claimed—the place of skulls—was to be found in the Garden Tomb, a sunlit green space outside the walls of the Old City, next to some cliffs that could wishfully be described as skull-like.

Many of the foreign tour guides here seemed to be preachers or professors, eager to pass on their versions of the truth; most of the local tour operators were grizzled, caustic men in their late fifties, in cowboy hats and heavy jeans, commanding an air of undeludedness.

"You see, there's a 'status quo contract' governing this church," one such guide was telling his four guests, "which lays down in very great detail the precise laws for worship. How many lamps each of the six groups can burn. Who owns every piece of furniture. Even that ladder"—he pointed to a hopeless-looking set of steps stranded on a ledge halfway up the building—"it belongs to the Armenians. And if the Catholics are meant to be finished with their ceremony at 2:07, and they're still singing at 2:08, when the Armenians start up, you're gonna see a fistfight. The holiest Christian place in the world, and that's what you get."

A gaunt Ethiopian woman was pulling out from a small black bag rich in Amharic crosses a tall, thin, white candle, to place on a ledge, before pushing her forehead against the church's entrance, and prostrating herself, fully, on the ground. A stout, thick-necked Nigerian man was reminding his large flock (the men all in "Praise the Lord" baseball caps, the women in brightly colored dresses), "We are not here for cha-cha. If the cha-cha comes out, it is the enemy. The Devil is waiting to make use of us!" The local guide, meanwhile, was pointing out two burly, mustachioed men seated on the steps next to the church's entrance and explaining how, by Saladin's decrees, it was two Muslim families who had controlled the keys of the Christian church for more than eight hundred years and locked the squabbling monks inside the space every evening.

And yet, the place was transfixing. It had none of the soaring archways or rose windows that transported me in the great cathedrals of Europe. It had none of the clarity and peace of even the light-filled Church of Saint Anne down the street. It wasn't restful or chaste or harmonious. It was simply raw and beyond, it seemed, all taming.

Jerusalem, more than anywhere I'd seen, was a city of words. Yet the single most moving sentence I'd registered so far had been posted just outside the Basilica of the Agony, not far from where a young nun stood at the gate, nibbling on an orange as she gazed into the distance.

"PLEASE," said the sign there, "No Explanations In-side the Church."

———

One morning, I decided to flee the contention of the shouting streets and travel out to Galilee, to see the places where Jesus had come of age. I found myself in the hands of a guide who might have been a model of the land around him: Amir was young, infectiously quick-witted and graced with a rare gift for cutting himself—for cutting everything—down to size.

He'd greeted our small group in Jerusalem by handing around a puzzle: looked at in one way, he pointed out, it resembled a mountain range; adjust your eyes, and you could make out a four-letter word.

That, apparently, was a metaphor for the holy city. And as for himself? Well, he said, shaking his tangle of black curls, he'd studied Judaism in Venezuela. But he'd gone on to master Catholicism in Trinidad. He'd researched Hinduism, for some reason, along the Ganges. And every stop surely quickened a pinwheeling gift for debate that was no doubt his from the beginning.

As we arrived in Nazareth, after a very long drive, someone in our group asked the inevitable question: how could one ever solve the problem of a country in which two opposing groups both have fair claim to the land beneath their feet? So many centuries converged here that a precedent could be found for almost anything.

"It's not a problem," said Amir, imperturbable. "It's an issue. A problem you can solve. An issue you have to live with."

So it was hopeless even to think of a solution?

"We've been coexisting, not always peacefully, for thousands of years," he continued. "So long as no one tries to solve their problems, they'll be okay."

With that, he started reaching for the kind of reassurances I'd heard at interfaith gatherings in every corner of the globe: all religions are different paths to the summit of the same mountain.

"It's like we have Windows 95," he went on—I remembered now that he'd said he'd completed his religious education by studying computers in Houston—"and the Christians have Windows 2.0. The Muslims have Vista."

But if that metaphor held, then surely some software engineer in Tel Aviv could come up with an open-source solution that might make the programs compatible?

"It's all the same system," he concluded, "but they think we're outdated. And you can't run our software on their machines."

Yet religion is dealing in absolutes, I thought, and even Steve Jobs didn't make that claim for his computers; they were in fact predicated on the idea of permanent progress, and relativity.

By the end of the day, after so many sites and debates, we were exhausted.

"You're looking confused," said our indefatigable guide, scanning our tired faces. "Are you feeling frustrated and confused?"

We were, a few of us confessed.

"You mean you know even less than when the day began?"

We did, in parts.

Amir lit up. "If I've left you feeling frustrated and confused," he exclaimed with delight, "I've succeeded! Now you know what it's like to be an Israeli! I've lived here for thirty-one years and still I don't know what's going on. In fact I know less and less. The more I learn, the more I can see how little I know."

Sometimes, in the sunlit silence of my room in the Austrian Hospice, I thought of the Benedictine hermitage in California that had been my secret home for almost seventeen.years. As soon as I stepped into my simple room there, something in me grew quiet. The arguments, the anxieties of the long drive up disappeared. In the ringing silence—no telephones, no internet, no television—my attention was brought to a point. All I could see was the great blue plate of the Pacific Ocean stretching below me in every direction, the Steller's jays alighting on a splintered wooden fence.

Days, sometimes weeks, in the silence had given me a taste of what lies on the far side of our thoughts. Who we become—cease to become—when we put all ideas and theories behind us. I went often through pages of Thomas Merton there, but they seemed to belong to the cacophony below the stillness; the golden pampas grass in front of me, the dry hills beyond, the fleecy clouds stealing up the hillside—not what I thought about them—were the truth.

The monastery far above the ocean had given me a rich sense of community because everyone I met there had come in search of the same silence and clarity; we were bound together by what was deepest in us. It didn't matter if the person I passed along the monastery road was Jewish or

Muslim or Buddhist; we were all walking in the same direction.

One day, as I'd been sauntering along the silent path, gazing out at the blue-green sea pooling around rocks far below, a young man with dark hair and burning eyes called out a hello. His name was Jonathan, he said, and he'd been living with the monks inside their enclosure for two years. They'd given him permission to stay with them, observing the Sabbath in his kippah and drawing from their air of worship and collectedness, and he in return did some baking in the kitchen, odd jobs around the property.

He looked out across the wide blue horizons as we spoke. There were only two places he'd found that brought him to a deeper life, he said: this elemental coastline, whose sovereign presences were rock and tree and ocean and sky, and Jerusalem. Years later, I wasn't surprised to learn that Jonathan had followed his instinct back to that ancestral home, and one afternoon I arranged to meet him in the Old City, near where he was studying to be a rabbi.

Around us, at the entrance to the tunnels at the Western Wall, disappointed visitors were cursing and pushing at the middle-aged cashier who barred their entrance—she unhesitatingly pushed them back—while out in the streets of West Jerusalem, I might have been back at an American college town on a Saturday night: "See, that's cool. Because when *my* dad got into new music it was, like, Shakira. And I was, like, What's with that?"

"Two thousand years of exile and we end up with this?" asked Jonathan, in one of Jerusalem's distinctive, and irresistible, voices.

We took dinner in a simple soup restaurant, and I heard about his studies. I thought a little of Oxford again, as I heard about the rigorous steeping in texts, the training in argumentation, the virtuoso ratiocination so far from what he'd seen when he'd looked out across the Pacific. Would this really be an advance, I thought: to dissect and find reasons for what had come to him as suddenly as sunlight? Would not argument lead to counterargument, assertion to rebuttal? To grasp the life of the spirit through study sounded like trying to read Homer by learning German. "The universes which are amenable to the intellect," I'd read in *The Cloud of Unknowing*, "can never satisfy the instincts of the heart."

Still, I knew I couldn't look away from the contention, in the streets and in the head; it was Melville who had reminded the hopeful spirits of his time that to look away from jails and hospitals was to denigrate humanity. So, my penultimate night in Jerusalem, I took the long, six-mile trip to Bethlehem, braving the checkpoints that seemed now to exile it from the Holy Land: at one point, soldiers with their guns at the ready clambered onto the bus, checking papers, and a professorial man in jacket and tie was hustled away, never to return.

When at last we edged into the city I'd been hearing about since I was a five-year-old playing Joseph in a Christmas pageant, I saw policemen patrolling the rooftops around Manger Square. In the Church of the Nativity, as at the church that I'd made my own in Jerusalem, the Copts gathered in one corner, Ethiopians were busily preparing for a midnight vigil in another and a Greek Orthodox priest in the pulpit was trying to drown out both parties with some readings.

I watched a Coptic monk sidle up to a pale, shy-looking Franciscan.

"You know," he began, "I was in America when you had that attack from the Greeks. And I thought, Idiots! Bastards! They're bastards! What kind of spiritual mission is this?"

The Franciscan smiled weakly, and the preparations for worship went on.

———

My final day in Jerusalem, I went back, as if by compulsion, to the rooftop of the Church of the Holy Sepulchre just as the last golden light was catching the Russian Orthodox gable, the Lutheran bell tower, the crosses of Greece, Armenia and Rome. A small woman was pressing her ear against the grating on the dome of the Chapel of St. Helena below, to catch the chants rising faintly from the candled space. The thump of Arabic music emerged from one of the houses nearby. The cries of kids playing in an alleyway blended with hymns sung by nuns behind the walls of their convent.

Incense drifted up through the cross-shaped grating on the small dome. On the worn, crooked green doors that led to the Ethiopian monks' cells, I saw the crosses that might have seemed all the renunciates had to sustain themselves with.

I walked down the narrow stairs then, through contested St. Michael's Chapel, and past the four grave priests, resting on their staffs, holding candles to their Bibles. I wandered across the courtyard and into the sacred center of everything. Large groups of Russians were everywhere, as the Orthodox Christmas drew closer, kneeling down to kiss the slab at the entrance, pushing crosses and medallions and talismans down upon it.

Pasty-faced men who could have passed for Vladimir Putin's cousins were pressing their lips to the cold, thick pillars. Yellow-haired Natashas in tracksuits cut open towards the navel were posing in front of flashbulbs near the sanctum sanctorum. Teenage girls were bearing bowls of incense, fanning the dim candles that flickered around the darkened space into small flames.

I headed back to the place that had become my own—"Christ's Prison"—and sat in the bare, chill space, in front of the small candle that someone had placed again on the stony ledge. As ever, there was something here, in the very neglectedness, that I could not explain away. I'd been sitting there for a long time—all thoughts of time dissolved—when a French girl, maybe fourteen, with thick glasses beneath a tumble of black curly hair, walked past and stopped as she saw the candle.

She didn't move for a very long time. She looked and looked at the candle, so small and ready to gutter out. She began to sob.

A friend arrived and held her close. The girl received the comfort for a few moments, weeping freely, and together they began to walk away. Then she stopped and turned to look again at the candle, eyes glistening. The thin light flickered and wavered, and somehow continued to burn.

The Morning of
the World

I was back in the beginning of the world, I thought, as my new friend Phunchok eased our rickety white Toyota over the "highest motorable pass in the world," at 18,380 feet, and, finally, down a single-lane path into a silent valley. Marmots scrambled across the asphalt; in the far distance Phunchok pointed out kiang, or wild asses. A vast flat plain stretched towards the Himalayan snowcaps. Here and there, small patches of green allowed sturdy white buildings to stand in the shelter of apricot trees and willows.

We passed two-humped Bactrian camels foraging among the sand dunes, silhouetted against a sky so blue, it almost hurt to look at it. Dry riverbeds were etched against sculpted rock formations.

Then we rounded a turn and suddenly, high above, stood a gompa, or Ladakhi temple. Like most of the gompas

I'd seen, it trembled on top of a hill as if fallen from the pocket of some absentminded god. Phunchok stopped the car, and we clambered up, to find ourselves in a rich and barely lit Tibetan Buddhist compound. Its chapels were thick with the smell of centuries of melted yak butter; its white terraces looked out upon mile after mile of noise-less valley.

Ladders led up to rooftops that dropped off into an almost allegorical landscape of sand and space and blue emptiness. Every door through which we passed led to thangkas swarming with skulls, furious depictions of the contest within each one of us of light and dark. Mandalas, often sacred diagrams representing a paradise of Buddhas, lined up in rows or arrayed in receding squares, presented maps for every visitor to awaken a Buddha inside. If king-doms in the Himalayas seem to belong to an earlier time, that may be in part because their citizens have never lost a sense of living within a field of spirits far beyond our reckon-ing. The human is a tiny thing on an encompassing canvas.

We sat in the silence, undisturbed, till at last we heard footsteps, some harried breathing. It was a Tibetan, it turned out, a friendly photographer now based in Kabul. He caught his breath and looked across the scene all around: the houses gathered in clusters in the dry valley down below, the snow on the barren mountains, the peace that passeth understanding.

"I could be back in Afghanistan," he said at last, alluding to the land that has thwarted every kind of invader.

————

So what, I wondered as we headed back to town, could I bring to this dry, quiet region in northern India often referred to as "the world's last Shangri-La"? Yes, I felt invigorated—uplifted and beautifully simplified—in the high, clear air of Ladakh; but what did it, with its air of self-containment, have to gain from me? In *Lost Horizon*, the 1930s book and film that had first spread the idea of Shangri-La—a sanctuary of "peace and security" hidden within the Himalayas—the four Westerners who stumble into the enchanted valley bring anger and restlessness and guns.

Phunchok, my red-cheeked, constantly smiling new companion, had grown up much as generations of his forebears had done, amid fields of barley and wheat irrigated by glacial snowmelt. Ladakh was free of much of the cataract poverty and displacement that left more than one hundred thousand children struggling to survive on the streets of Mumbai alone. Barely 235,000 souls occupied the largest union territory in all of enormous India, and even when I'd first heard the name in high school, it was hardly connected to the outside world by reliable roads.

So even to set foot here could feel like a kind of trespass.

If Ladakh was content, would not any change represent a loss? Yes, it remains a decidedly real-world location, where Indian troops clash with Chinese and face off against Pakistani soldiers at twenty thousand feet. Just under the widely advertised highest motorable pass in the world, I'd come upon an entire Indian Army encampment; a uniformed Sikh had checked my identity while a helicopter circled overhead, as if to remind me that I hadn't left reality behind at all.

The entire region, in fact, was governed by Srinagar, the tense and unsettled Kashmiri capital only 150 miles away as the crow flies. Yet into this precarious zone every summer came the most rigorous spokesman for peace I knew, the Fourteenth Dalai Lama, to remind fellow Buddhists that paradise can be found only in the middle of what's around us. Shangri-La exists exclusively in the imagination, he would say—and the word itself, it's often asserted, is a corruption of "Shambhala," referring to a mythical Tibetan kingdom that stands for a state of mind. Real life can offer us pleasures that fantasy leaves out.

———

It takes a while to adjust to elevation. As soon as my plane from Delhi touched down, I made my way to a guesthouse outside the small capital, Leh, and took to my bed. For two days and nights, I barely shifted, not quite here, but not exactly elsewhere. In some limbo, perhaps, in which I left behind one way of living and prepared for another.

Once I could easily breathe again, I moved into town and took a long walk down Main Bazaar Road, at the heart of the compact, bustling settlement. Women were seated across the sidewalks, selling vegetables, while skullcapped, white-bearded sheikhs assembled around the mosque not far away. The emerald eyes and fair complexions all around spoke of Samarkand, Turkestan, Herat. The first illusion I had to dispel was that Ladakh was a magically preserved province of Himalayan Buddhism; half its citizens were, I now learned, Muslim and for centuries it had been a trading post through which merchants passed, bearing silk and indigo, opium and gold, to Kashmir, Kashgar and other caravan stops along the Silk Road.

This meant, of course, that, like any busy intersection, it had lived for centuries off foreign influences. I shouldn't have been surprised that *Pirates of the Caribbean: At World's End* was being projected on a giant video screen in the garden restaurant down the street, days after its premiere at Disneyland. Or that Israeli travelers in harem pants were gathering around a flyer that advertised a full-moon party. A "paradise on earth" can remain itself only by changing with the times.

I went to dinner, very early in my stay, with a British

anthropologist who had been working in the region off and on for a decade. Had things altered much over the time he'd spent here? I asked. He didn't seem to think so. The Ladakhis had worked out centuries ago how to deal with the larger world, and how to keep their land relatively pure precisely by keeping its doors open. Every winter, as tourists faded away, the locals presented themselves to the Indian Army, worked through the cold season at the Siachen Glacier and stayed solvent till late spring opened tourist doors again.

Enterprise was hardly the enemy of innocence; it could even be its lifeline. Recently, the scholar informed me, the government in Kashmir had decreed that something be done about the packs of wild dogs running free around Ladakh. Instantly, the citizens of Leh had hurried out to place tags on every dog they saw, so that the animals would be taken to be pets and not hauled away or killed. Many never forgot that even a dog might be their mother in a past life—or a future one.

———

Next morning, I woke up thinking of Thoreau. When first I'd met his bracing words, at the age of twenty-one, I'd heard the firm, commonsensical sound of a voice that came to me like something I knew, but had somehow misplaced. "A man is rich in proportion to the number of things which he can afford to let alone." Might not simplicity confer on us a freedom that complexity could never bring? "I have always been regretting," he wrote, in words that stirred a sense of recognition, "that I was not as wise as the day I was born."

Thoreau is often credited with helping to bring many of the great texts of the East into a modern American vernacular, the Vedas of Hinduism and the foundations of Buddhism among them. But what brought him to mind here in Leh, at some level deeper than conscious thought, was that he was always singing a new morning. There was a freshness, a sense of undistractedness, in these Himalayan spaces I'd never found at similar altitudes in the Altiplano or the Rockies. I woke to the sound of chopping wood. The cries of runny-nosed children rang out along the mud-walled alleyways. Women were hanging washing from a rooftop as the high, clear sunshine seemed to announce the dawning of the world.

This sense of a pristine order was difficult to resist, and I'd felt it outside the Potala Palace in 1985 and traveling across Bhutan, as well as living among the foothills of the Himalayas in Dharamsala for several springs. But here in Ladakh an entire society seemed to be suggesting that progress meant continuity, and remoteness could make for a kind of intimacy.

I stepped up into my seat beside Phunchok at first light,

and my cheerful friend drove us around the enormous prayer wheels that stand near the center of Leh, to confer blessings on every car that leaves the capital. We accelerated past the "War Hero Filling Station" and out into the open country-side, which began within seconds. Phunchok thrust a worn cassette of local folk songs into his sound system, and as a single-string, piercing nomad ballad filled the car, he turned to me and flashed a craggy, enormous smile.

Twenty minutes on, we looked up and saw a gompa, as ever perilously perched upon a mountain. *Gompa* means "solitary place," yet each of these mountain fastnesses was so rich in color, and in this case so thick with the presence of recently completed chants, that it was hard to feel lonely, even in the emptiness. Every dawn now was bringing some fresh liberation: two days before, we'd gone to the cele-brated monastery at Hemis, which seemed somehow to have been carved out of the hillside that shelters it; yester-day to the temple at Rizong, hidden by folds in a mountain that, for the locals, suggest the folds of a monk's robes.

Later to Alchi, a quiet village of running streams and cozy houses, where we walked among Kashmiri murals in temples surrounded by apricot and apple trees. Even within this faraway land places seemed doubly sheltered by geol-ogy; Ladakh's central town might have been entertaining visitors for centuries, but in the countryside, we were back in a region that had not seen street lighting when Bill Clinton arrived in the White House.

To get to Lamayuru, we had to drive through great clefts in the mountain, ocher and purple and brown, on a one-lane road that wends its way for many hours up above a river eighteen hundred feet below. For a long time we saw no other cars. As we pulled up to its entrance—who knew when the last visitor had come through?—I glimpsed a sign: "Welcome to Moon Land View."

In front of us was a hauntingly irregular scatter of white-walled, red-fringed temples and chapels and schools, extending across the sand-colored rock like a city on a hill. We got out of the car and a grubby monk emerged from a doorway, bearing a huge and ancient-looking key. I handed him a few pennies, as Phunchok had advised, and the boy in robes led me from one massively padlocked prayer hall to the next.

Shafts of sunlight streamed in from above, picking out dusty thangkas fluttering above rows of prayer cushions. Bulging-eyed black demons copulated on murals, while golden Buddhas sat serenely in the diagram's corners; it might have been a vision of the struggle for not just my soul but that of the entire world. Feet cold on the bare floor, I stepped out again into the blustery sunshine, to hear nothing but the snapping of prayer flags in a brisk wind.

"Life is boring in Leh," a campsite owner in the Nubra Valley had explained to me, as if to give voice to what I might be thinking, translating his terms into mine. "But in America, I think, busy, busy, busy, twenty-four/seven. So much tension. Stress, stress, stress."

When he stopped, there was silence.

"So American people come here for peace, contentment. Weather is hot and cold, everything is boring—but life is good here."

He sounded uncannily similar to the cheerful residents of Shangri-La in *Lost Horizon*, never slow to proclaim that their realm is a kind of clinic for the distressed. At its climax the film turns upon a rending choice, worthy of a thangka, between the pure, hidden world that calls to the protagonist and the summons of a war-torn reality far below.

James Hilton's book remained unexpectedly attuned to the Buddhism of the region it evoked (even as it ascribed those principles to Christians): its central notion claimed that "perhaps you've always been a part of Shangri-La without knowing it." Yet it's in the nature of a hospital to get crowded with the infirm, often contagious in their unease.

"Oh, I just wish the whole world might come to this valley," one guileless inhabitant cries in her unfallen state of grace. "Then," says one of the recently arrived, "it wouldn't be a garden spot for long."

———

Whenever I spoke with the Dalai Lama—often for days at a time, as I ended up traveling with him across Japan on ten trips in twelve years, by his side for every hour of his working day—I was struck anew by his realism. As leader of his people since the age of four, he had no interest in wishful or romantic notions; true to the example of what he called his "big boss," the Buddha, he always seemed to see himself as a doctor of the mind. No physician is immortal, or infallible; none can save us from sickness or old age or death. All he can do is try to bring a clear and undeluded eye to our condition to see how he can ease some suffering.

Part of this medical model meant that he never suggested that one belief system was truer than any other. He characteristically likened religious traditions to medical systems, aware that Western doctors have expertise in certain areas, Tibetan doctors in others; for his own health he took pains to consult physicians from both traditions. It reminded me of how the Nobel-winning psychologist Daniel Kahneman maintained that we shouldn't concentrate on cultivating happiness so much as on relieving pain—that was the world's most urgent concern. In almost half a century of talking to the Dalai Lama, I'd never really heard him speak about Paradise (or Nirvana); such ideas could only be a distraction from the possibilities of real life.

This haunted me as I walked around the region he loved so much. The minute I'd landed in the airport at Leh, I'd been greeted by signs instructing me in the principles of "mindful tourism." Pamphlets advised me to "avoid buying products from multinational corporations . . . which are destroying local economies the world over." Mindfulness is generally preferable to its opposite, but I couldn't help wondering how the locals felt about the pieces of paper fluttering from every lamppost: "Say No to Polythene." Were we foreigners trying to protect Ladakhis from the parts of our culture we happened not to like? Did we imagine we were wiser than they, especially when it came to the business (which they had been negotiating for centuries) of dealing with foreign cultures? And might we not, in our very longing for paradise, be seeking to deny the residents of the place we romanticized the opportunities (to learn about other cultures and to be up-to-the-minute) that we found so indispensable ourselves?

One day, walking away from the center of Leh, I found myself very soon on a shaded rustic lane where villagers who looked as their great-grandparents might have done were making their slow, reverent way to the nearest temple. A group of musicians sat on the ground among the poplars, serenading a traditional archery competition: a team of elegant men in black appeared to be taking on a team in white. Scores were written up on a blackboard. Every break in the action brought a ceremonial dance.

As I went along the fields—villagers were singing as they worked—I remembered how the Dalai Lama, with his emphasis on facts and empiricism, often suggested that the seclusion of Himalayan cultures had perhaps allowed them to develop skills in meditation that had resulted in spiritual technologies not so refined yet in the West. But whenever someone asked him why Tibet was enduring such miseries now, he answered, without hesitation, that its biggest problem had been its isolation. If places such as Ladakh were to remain too far from the world, they could end up as neglected as Tibet had been when Mao Zedong's troops swept across the border in 1949 and none of the rest of the planet seemed to care.

His culture needed to be part of the larger world, he always stressed; he worked ceaselessly to bring modern Western science to the twelve thousand Buddhist monks who lived in India and he traveled from Silicon Valley to Mongolia to see how other cultures were navigating the shift to modernity. The core of Buddhist thinking was interdependence—"Indra's Net," as it's been called—and for a culture or a person to be cut off from others was to condemn it to a kind of nonexistence.

Whenever someone stood up—this happened after

almost every large public lecture—and asked him what to do after you've been disappointed in some dream (to bring peace to the Middle East, to reverse climate change, to protect some seeming idyll), the Dalai Lama looked over at the questioner with great warmth and said, "Wrong dream!" You have to analyze, research real causes and conditions and take the long view, he always stressed, before coming up with any plan. Pursuing an unrealistic dream was an insult to reality, as well as to dreamer and to dream.

———————

I thought of this soon after, at the Tsechu Festival in Hemis, one of the great events of the Ladakhi calendar. All around the great monastery sharp-cheeked men and women had gathered to sell turquoise necklaces, Buddha statues, thangkas and CDs. It took a Ladakhi to point out to me that the only eager consumers of such stuff were tourists; the few locals in evidence clustered around two homemade roulette wheels set among the trees.

Inside the temple's central courtyard, masked lamas were slowly raising their feet up and placing them down, again and again, again, in a deliberate set of meditative movements commemorating the great eighth-century "second Buddha" who brought Tantric Buddhism to Tibet, Padmasambhava. At least ninety percent of the visitors, I noticed, were fellow foreigners, unable to follow any of the symbolic action, though glad, I was sure, to see dances consecrated to the famous teacher.

"It used to be that all us young boys would go to Tsechu and make a big party," Tsewang Dorje, the winning and urbane young proprietor of Yak Travels, back in Leh, informed me. "Now it's only for the tourists." Indeed, many of Ladakh's festivals, traditionally held in winter, have been moved to the summer season so they can attract global crowds.

Would it be better, I wondered, if I'd never come at all, and if the many foreigners who had in some ways awakened Ladakhis to the beauties of their own culture were to stop coming? Or might the absence of outsiders in fact lead to a fading of local interest in traditional medicine as well as a falling off of resources? Even to a sense among the young that they had to abandon their homeland if they wished to be in touch with the possibilities of the modern world?

A hundred years ago, the British soldier Francis Younghusband (on whose experience, I sometimes thought, the story of Shangri-La had been based) had found Ladakhis to be "typical travelling merchant[s] of Central Asia . . . intelligent, shrewd, full of information." They knew, he sensed, how to take what they needed from every passing culture and, in so doing, to become only more themselves. They also knew—and it offered hope for Kashmir nearby, and

Jerusalem, and many of the places I visited—how to sustain several religious traditions at the same time without a huge amount of friction. There might be ads for cell phones on every red and white umbrella on the rooftop "Pizza de Hut" restaurant, but there was also a sign outside its entrance, "Thanks for the Visit. God Bless You. Take Care. Bye-Bye."

One evening I slipped off the main street, slithered through a passageway and, in a back lane, labored up some stairs to the comfy, carpeted Desert Rain coffeehouse. This full-moon evening, everyone in the place was Ladakhi except for me; most seemed to be excited teenage girls back for the holidays from their private schools in the plains, eager to thrash out the intricacies of Brad and Britney. Onstage a bespectacled Ladakhi boy was struggling his way through a rendition of "The Times They Are a-Changin'" The girls sang along with every word. They even lit up to see a fifty-two-year-old, dark-skinned visitor who'd clearly come from far away. What did I do for a living? one asked. From where did I come? "Can I write to you?" "Do you have a business card?"

It was the age-old exchange of Leh, I thought, the Silk Road in its latest form: I could offer up an explanation of what that line in "Life in the Fast Lane" meant, and they could tell me about their grandmother's experience of Padmasambhava. I had something that they wanted—a whiff

of the revved-up future—as much as they offered me a liberation from all of that. The owner of the place turned out
to be a friendly Mennonite from Colorado, bringing her
own kind of promised land to this Buddhist-Muslim world,
perhaps.

When Phunchok and I had finally arrived at the end of
our five-hour drive over the "highest motorable pass in the
world," it was to learn that (after all that effort) the gompa
in Hunder was closed. "During this time," someone in a
local village who knew a little English told us, "the head
monk is not here." "Why?" "This season so many insects
die," came the answer. "So they are making prayers for
them in all the houses."

I looked then at my tireless driver, who had showed
up morning after morning without complaint, at dawn or
earlier, to take us both on hazardous trips along unpaved
roads. Until four years ago, he had never left his nomad
settlement, where he and his neighbors lived by the seasons; even now, he could not read or write. Since he had
come to town, though, and begun working with a travel
agency, he had been able to send his seventeen-year-old boy
to private school in Delhi, where, much like the girls listening to the Eagles, he was learning English, economics and
all the skills of the modern world.

I came to know this because the son joined us one day
on our travels, dressed in a Nike shirt and baseball cap,

fluent in English. My presence had given him the perfect chance to visit his own culture.

When we stopped in at a temple, it was he, not his father, who ensured that I circumambulate in the right, propitious direction; it was he, in fact, who threw himself down on the ground in full prostrations before every Buddha. It was the urban, worldly-wise son, as we stopped for lunch, who insisted that we eat only in temple-sponsored restaurants. His summer vacation, he told me, was devoted entirely to visiting the nomad camp of his ancestors, and learning everything he could never learn in school.

Then he got back into the Toyota and let his father drive the foreigner—and his karmically blessed self—off to the next place of worship. By then, I'd stopped wondering how much this was the future or the past. The two sturdy souls beside me in the car seemed to have little thought about living in "Shangri-La"—and much more about making the real world as rich as possible.

A Lotus in Mud

All night long—I might have been in Broome again—
the ocean surged and pounded a few yards from my
room. I got up in the dark, from my four-poster bed, and
went over to open the window. The clasp at the bottom
was so new, it refused to give. I pushed and prodded, till at
last it moved a little, and then I took up the fight with the
lock at the top. Finally, the panes flew open and admitted
a rush of wind. Minutes later, the papers I'd placed on the
desk began to curl.

Before long, heavy rain began slashing through the
open frame and when I made my way, scratchy and tired,
that first morning in Sri Lanka, to the verandah, overlooking the gardens of the 140-year-old hotel, it was to find that
every last table and chair had been cleared away. The smell
of salt was everywhere; even inside the once-grand dining

room, I could hear the ocean thudding against the shore, its spray catching me at intervals.

I let the downpour play itself out, and then, fresh fruit and toast behind me, I walked out through the hotel's pillared entrance, to where buses and three-wheelers were thundering through the heart of the busy capital. Just across the way was the glorious stretch of green running along the sea I'd seen in all the posters: Galle Face Green.

Children were flying kites in the brightening midsummer morning, as in travel agents' photos. Lovers were snuggling closer under the cover of umbrellas. A man was approaching a group of picnickers to see if anyone was in need of a fake beard. Across the lawn a toddler was being handed a pink balloon, and then a blown-up Spider-Man. Just above the little boy, however, helicopters kept hovering. Between every palm tree armed soldiers were posted, twenty-one in all. All of central Colombo—the area known as "Fort"— was cut up and crisscrossed by roadblocks till I could no longer tell whether I was being kept in or out.

Not far away, as I wandered around the central area, was the hospital where a pregnant woman, a few weeks earlier, had blown up several civilians with a bomb tucked against her expanding stomach. Over there was the president's residence—"Temple Trees," as it was lyrically styled—in which the warmongering leader was barricaded behind signs reading HIGH SECURITY ZONE. I stepped into the Hilton and felt like the only suspect in a detective story. Were my Tamil features the problem? No, I decided: in an island on permanent alert, everyone was presumed guilty until proven otherwise.

By the time I got back to the restored wing of my hotel—a sign in the lobby announced its arrival on *Condé Nast Traveler*'s "Hot List"—all electricity was gone. I wandered down darkened corridors, but nobody was in sight. A rat scuttled across the bar, not far from the plaque recalling some of the ghosts who had inhabited the place: Japan's wartime emperor; Richard Nixon; Ingrid, Queen of Denmark.

When I returned to my honeymoon suite, there was nothing to do but pick up a book. The ocean in its pages hammered against rocks just as it was doing right here. Finally, as darkness fell, the lights flickered back to life and I went out to the hotel's expansive lawns, where a large white tent had been set up for a wedding reception. The lead singer of a four-piece band was cheerfully warning, "You can't hide your lyin' eyes." Men in dark suits and women in golden saris mingled.

Then, as I watched, one of the men slipped away from the festivities and headed towards the hotel bar. A large-screen television there was showing the Sri Lankan team thump the English in the white-flannel gentleman's sport the English had brought them. Then another fugitive slipped away, then a third.

Minutes later, a young woman in a billowing pink dress, thick, scented hair falling to her waist, came into the room where the men had gathered and took a seat at the bar. Several pairs of eyes followed her. Was she another refugee from the wedding party, or a visitor from the street? Tamil or Sinhalese? A product of the war, or of the hope for re-gaining paradise in spite of it?

And what exactly were the men's intentions, I wondered, as they began to circle the lone pink dress, and I tried to figure out where exactly I'd ended up.

———

It had seemed the perfect moment, when first I planned the trip, to visit the paradise island. After more than twenty years of bitter fighting between the separatist Tamil Tigers, agitating for their own independent homeland, and the ruling Sinhalese government, a cease-fire had finally been declared, thanks in part to the intercession of Norway. Bou-tique hotels began sprouting along the palmy coast; foreign-ers started snapping up old houses along Galle's picturesque narrow lanes and turning them into trendy galleries. Sri Lanka had been through many convulsions before, yet its reputation for sea-sweetened idyll had always returned.

One day after Christmas, however, six seasons earlier,

the ocean had come in and in, never receding. "Sea covered sea," as Adam witnessed in *Paradise Lost*, "sea without shore." By the time the tsunami subsided, thirty-six thousand people on the island were gone. Almost half a million were without a home. Slowly, painfully, the island began to pick itself up again, and then the Tamils decided that this was the perfect moment to break the cease-fire. A hard-line party of militant Sinhalese roared back into power and the fighting resumed with fresh intensity.

"Now," said a droll friend, "your stay should be even more absorbing." The feeling was that reality had more dimensions than paradise could ever accommodate.

———

The jungle comes into the house in Sri Lanka: every book I'd read about the island had evoked that passage. Jesus lizards, nightjars, brain-fever birds were everywhere, Michael Ondaatje wrote in his classic memoir about returning to the land where he was born; often, growing up, he could not say whether he was indoors or out. Biblical downpours, the scent of cinnamon, the serpents (traditionally left unharmed on the island): all of them turn every division inside out. Settlers from Europe had erected columned palaces to try to keep the jungle at bay—this is the

sad strain at the edge of his story—but always some wild-
ness rose up again to overwhelm them. The author's father was found running naked through the streets; private
affairs slipped into public view; attempts at "civilization"
proved flimsy in the face of monsoonal storms and the creep
and chatter of the wild.

Leonard Woolf, living on the island for almost seven
years as a civil administrator with a rare sympathy for his
new neighbors, came to fear the jungle, and all the darkness
that he sensed it housed. One night he ended up stranded
amid the trees and refused to sleep, lest spirits or beasts
carry him off; Jan Morris, unblushingly in love with "Ser-
endib," admitted that the murder rate here was among the
highest in the world when she rhapsodized about the place
in 1967. D. H. Lawrence savored the beauty of the island,
but—as in many places—he went almost mad during his
month in the Buddhist capital, Kandy, where he encountered the visiting Prince of Wales, but also coconut torches,
"tom-toms and savage music and devil dances," a primal
intensity that gave him a "glimpse into the world before
the Flood." After leaving the island, he felt like "Virgil in
the Shades."

In the guidebooks, a fourteenth-century papal legate
was often cited. "From Seylan to Paradise . . . is a distance
of forty Italian miles," he wrote back to the Vatican, and
"'tis said you can hear the sound of the water of its foun-

tains there." Within earshot of the Garden, but not inside it: it had the feeling of the loneliest location in the world.

———

Yet right at the heart of the country lay the Buddhist sites that had awakened in pilgrims for centuries the notion of a better world, by way of a clearer self. And what had really brought me here was something very private: I wanted to see the place that had overwhelmed Thomas Merton, the English-raised monk whose books I read daily as if they were my own secret diary.

Merton had not set foot outside the United States for almost twenty-seven years when he boarded a plane in San Francisco in 1968 to fly to Asia; after nearly half a lifetime in a silent cloister in Kentucky, he devoured every detail of his journey with a poignant intensity. Arriving in India, he gave himself over to a series of discussions with the thirty-four-year-old Dalai Lama, the Tibetan as excited to exchange meditation practices with a Christian monk as Merton was to encounter Buddhism in the flesh. Then he made his way down to Sri Lanka, at the time known as Ceylon.

He stayed on arrival, just as I was doing, amid the "faded cream splendor" of the Galle Face Hotel, chafing against the American songs being played, often right underneath his room, and the local girl who introduced herself as "Heather." He walked around the area named Fort and noted, even then, "everywhere there are police and military, very aggressive, with sharp fixed bayonets or machine guns even." He watched children flying kites on Galle Face Green and took the early train to Kandy, claiming a seat in a carriage reserved "For Clergy Only."

Finally, after seeing the rock caves at Dambulla, where a guide pointed out a representation of "Tamils being chopped up in war"—amid rows of meditating Buddhas— he came to the great ruined city of Polonnaruwa. The Christian vicar general with whom he was traveling had no interest in the pagan forms of Buddhism, but Merton stepped up to the twenty-three-foot figure standing beside a reclining, forty-six-foot Buddha—Siddhartha on his deathbed—and was transformed.

"The silence of the extraordinary faces," he wrote. "The great smiles." They seemed to be seeing past every question without discrediting a thing. "There is no puzzle, no problem and really no 'mystery,'" he concluded. He could not even put his feelings into words till days later, he had been so profoundly affected: "I know and have seen what I was obscurely looking for." Less than a week thereafter, returning to his room in Bangkok for lunch after delivering a lecture on Marxism and monasticism, the wandering monk was found dead, apparently electrocuted by a fan.

It was striking to me that Merton had found what he needed in the cessation of all questions, even if that would never be the same thing as answers; I remembered how he'd written that to have all the answers might be proof that you weren't asking the right questions. Uncertainty was perhaps the place where all of us—even a monk—have to make our home. But I was also moved that a man who had devoted his life to the Christian God had been so stirred by faces of the Buddha, as if heaven was not the private property of any group.

Very soon, therefore, I quit the roadblocks of the capital for the Buddhist center, on what might have been the same slow and rusty train that had once transported Merton. The first row of my carriage still said "For Clergy," though in contemporary Sri Lanka, that could carry a divisive sound; in Colombo's station, even certain restrooms had been set aside for clergy. The waiting rooms had been denominated, with quaint decorousness, "For Gentlemen" and "For Ladies."

I watched, much as Merton had done, women washing clothes—and themselves—in rivers along the way, children waving at the passing train. The schoolboys around me—"Seventeen years of age, sir!"—disarmed me with their innocence; as the carriage rattled on, we passed younger children in spotless white uniforms drifting down red-dirt lanes to class. I opened the local paper at the obituary section, and came across notices for a "Retired Locomotive Driver, Old Josephian," a "Retired Assistant Collector of Customs," an "ex Cricket Captain of Ananda College—1953." The yellowing names carried me back to a kind of golden age before the current war.

On arrival in Kandy, I stepped out to be greeted by what looked to be a quiet town built around a man-made lake: a perfect vision of Buddhist clarity and calm. Yet the central Temple of the Tooth, containing the country's most sacred relic (a tooth said to belong to the Buddha), remained such a tempting target for assault that, the minute I stepped in, the only visitor in sight, alarms began screaming and I was hustled out onto the streets again.

Anxious officials whispered orders into walkie-talkies; local buses were commandeered to block off the road.

I longed to place myself as far as possible from such unrest (and, besides, the celebrated tooth was said to belong to a dog, and not even on display). So I found a hotel up in the hills, where a smiling young local offered to drive me to the Buddhist sites next day. We set off early, to beat the heat, and a hundred or so minutes after leaving the roosters and chirruping birds announcing daybreak, we pulled into a parking lot outside Sigiriya, the 590-foot vertical rock often taken as a symbol of the nation all around.

A sign when I got out of the car announced the presence of killer bees. A man seated on the ground whipped the

cover off a wicker basket, and a cobra began slithering out
of its depths. "No need, no need," my driver cried; there'd
be plenty of poisonous serpents at the top.

It took me fully an hour to ascend the thirteen hundred
steps of the "Lion Rock," laboring alone over uncertain
stones while Italians around me cried, *"Bravissima!"* At
one point I found myself on a thin black spiral staircase. I
looked down: nothing between me and what looked like
the end, a very long way below.

At heart, I'm scared of only two things—heights and
snakes—and this emblem of Sri Lanka was bringing the
two together with terrifying intensity. "You see that iron
staircase?" a visitor from England was telling a companion.
"They brought it over from the London Underground. Seventy years ago. It's going to give out at any moment."

I slipped, and a pebble went flying towards the dust. I
tried not to look down towards the Islamic gardens at the
base, reproducing the four quarters of Paradise. At the
summit, a local hurried up, eager to show me terraces for
dancing and ornamental pools. I didn't really want to look
around, though looking around was the only reason to
make the long ascent.

"Do you see many accidents here?"

"Oh, too many, sir. Killer bees, some people slipping. So
many people too stupid."

Chameleons turned red in the sun—and white and

green—beside some sleeping pythons. Huge lizards that could have been iguanas—"land monitors," I heard—breathed heavily along the outcropping. Around me were the ruins of a fortress in the sky founded by a man who had stolen the throne, buried his father alive in the wall of a reservoir and then, betrayed by a fellow insurgent, slit his own throat.

As I began edging my way down the rock face again, somebody nearby reminded a friend that a descent is always the most dangerous part of a trip. The angriest devils in *Paradise Lost*, I recalled, are the ones who have fallen farthest. When at last I arrived, out of breath, at my car, it was to find the driver drumming his fingers against the hood; time was short, and we had too many other places to see today.

Back on the one-lane road, between cashew trees and mangoes, he floored the accelerator as if demons were on our tail. A truck came careening towards us, and, with less than a second to spare, he swerved out of its way, narrowly missing an overfull bus on our side of the road. Now a taxi from the other side was speeding into our lane, and each driver was daring the other to turn away first. I tried to keep my eyes away from the side of the road, where overturned cars lay here and there in ditches, abandoned trucks stood with their doors bashed in.

We sped into the area around Polonnaruwa, the royal

ruin that had turned Merton's life around, and a red-eyed man labored towards us, hand extended.

"Last year," he explained. "A motorcycle. I woke up in the hospital. No money. No bike."

I handed him a few coins—visitors were scarce—and walked on to see the Buddhas. They stared at me impassively. Onto the quiet faces in the sun I could project anything I needed. Our one task is to make friends with reality, I could imagine them whispering—which is to say, with impermanence and suffering and death; the unrest you feel will always have more to do with you than with what's around you. In one celebrated story, the Buddha had come upon a group of picnickers who were enraged because they'd just been robbed.

"Which," he'd famously asked, "is more important? To find the robbers or to find yourself?"

———

The struggle in a Buddhist world—I thought of the murals in the temples of Ladakh—is essentially believed to take place within. The notion of an external paradise is one of the main illusions and projections we have to sweep aside, as we might a sand mandala. As the driver and I walked together through the five cave temples at Dambulla, an enormous black rock that had housed a monastery two thousand years before, we passed lines of stone or sandalwood Buddhas, joined in places by some Hindu gods. We saw the Buddha sitting unmoved as the demon Mara tried to tempt him away from clarity; we saw him delivering his first discourse, in Sarnath, on the fact of suffering and the means to try to take care of it. For the Buddha, every other statue reminded us, the truest way to transform yourself came from sitting still.

By the time we emerged, the sun was beginning to descend, with tropical abruptness. We were encircled by trees. There were leopards in the jungle, the driver said, and elephants. The elephants were so dangerous that even truck drivers passed through in a convoy. Also, he said, guerrillas: they were everywhere.

We set off as quickly as we could, but, within minutes, our coughing Hyundai began to splutter and the driver eased it to the side of the road and turned off the faltering ignition.

We sat in the silence, awaiting the sound of threat.

"Is there someone you can call?"

He waved his aged cell phone at me. No battery.

"What do we do?"

My companion shrugged. At last, as night began to envelop us, he got out and trooped off under the darkening sky into the forest. Minutes later, he emerged again, a wildhaired figure behind him, bare-chested above his sarong.

The stranger pushed open the hood and fiddled and tweaked. The car coughed into a kind of life and the driver jumped in before it could expire again and revved up the tired engine.

Soon the red arrow was jittering near the far end of the speedometer. A truck was blaring its horn at us. A bus was overtaking a slow car and coming straight towards us. "It doesn't matter if we get back late," I assured my impatient friend. "We're in no hurry."

"I know, sir." He took both hands off the wheel to convey the urgency of the situation. "But no lights, sir. Now too dark."

It was indeed. The screaming buses and horn-blasting trucks were shining their lights right at us, but we were almost invisible to them in the night.

"I never have accident," protested the driver, turning around to assure me of his sincerity, as we surged past a lone bicycle wobbling in the dark.

"I did. Last year. In Bolivia. At thirteen thousand feet. I almost died."

"No problem, sir." The arrow on the speedometer seemed ready to explode.

"Do you live round here?"

"No, sir. So many time driving, driving." Sometimes, he said, he slept in the guerrilla camps, though whether as supporter or mere tourist chauffeur he did not specify.

"You have brothers and sisters?"

"One sister, sir." He turned around again, ignoring the cars racing towards us. "She dead. Four years already."

"I'm sorry."

"Yes, sir. Driver too many drinking, sir. Hit her on the road."

It was pitch black now; I could not even see the wild eyes beneath the pomaded hair, the smile that came on and off with displacing ease. Then we were pulling to the side of the road again, and the car was still.

As inexplicably as before, a man emerged from the chattering darkness as from a Lexus showroom; behind him I thought I could make out a barn, appointed with rusty hubcaps. He opened the hood and tugged at some wires. He prodded and pulled, then walked slowly back to his shed.

It was near midnight by the time we arrived at the hotel, and the mountain road that led us there, via a series of blind curves, was unlit. We'd heard that more than seven thousand extra soldiers were flooding into town in anticipation of the annual midsummer festival.

I said goodbye to my trusty companion at the entrance to the hotel, but it was evident that he didn't want to leave. "Tomorrow, sir?" he asked. "Again?"

I told him, with relief and regret, that I'd seen everything I needed and he opened the door of the car and got in. A Spider-Man figure was bursting out of the back window as he accelerated around blind switchbacks towards the road on which his sister had lost her life.

———

As in Kashmir, but more dramatically, Sri Lanka seemed to owe much of its sorrow to its centuries-old status as an earthly paradise. The "teardrop island"—this had become the newspapers' unvarying phrase—had been blessed with a perfect location along the sea-lanes that link the planet's hemispheres; it was said that the scent of cinnamon could, Circe-like, draw travelers to its shores. Arabs described the island as "contiguous with the Garden of Eden," and Galle, it was sometimes claimed, was Tarshish in the Bible, from which King Solomon collected elephants and peacocks and gemstones; later both Marco Polo and Ibn Battuta helped to lay the foundation for the tales that Sinbad the Sailor would spread of palaces encrusted with one hundred thousand rubies and spice trees. Alexander the Great is said to have sought the "elixir of life" in the lake he hoped to find on top of the holy mountain, Adam's Peak. Later it was the Portuguese, the Dutch, the British who sailed away with ginger and wild indigo and seven kinds of wild cinnamon; the "island of gems" was a rusty box with so many hands grabbing at the precious stones within that almost everyone was left dripping blood.

After the British claimed the island as one of their first Crown Colonies, early in the nineteenth century—more than four centuries under Portuguese, Dutch and then British rule was to be this Eden's unhappy fate—they began implementing their strategy of divide-and-rule, giving the hardworking and education-conscious Tamils, many of whom had learned English from missionaries, jobs as teachers and civil servants, even as the Sinhalese majority felt neglected. Yet by the time the island gained its independence, in 1948, its prospects looked golden: it enjoyed a free press, a spirited opposition, a literacy rate of more than fifty percent, amid all the blessings that Nature could confer. It was one of the richest countries in Asia. Eight years on, the government laid down, as if to avenge what had been done to them before, a "Sinhala Only" policy, and the Tamils, representing more than one in every five Sri Lankans but unable to speak the language of the Sinhalese, were rendered mute. Soon enough, they started to lobby for their own land, in which they could, quite literally, have a voice.

The fight that ensued, as described in Samanth Subramanian's brilliant book of reportage, *This Divided Island*, featured rare savagery on every side. The Tamils killed other Tamils who did not support their militancy. They forced every family to give up a child to the fighting and attacked Sinhalese pilgrims and monks. They pressured neighbors to don suicide vests; a woman in spectacles bent down to touch Rajiv Gandhi's feet, as the Indian prime minister was campaigning in the Indian state of Tamil Nadu, and detonated an explosive, and one more politician hoping to bring peace to a place of conflict was undone by violence.

On the other side, the Sinhalese turned to their holy book, the *Mahavamsa*, to find scriptural justification for the longing to exterminate Tamils; monks seized political power, as if their teacher had not shown that the only power that matters lies within. Nowadays, the violence was often prosecuted with the help of ancient cars that had created—I thought of my faltering vehicle on the way back from the Buddhas—a society of virtuoso mechanics.

In truth, the island had been a place of contention for more than two millennia by now, the Buddha's tooth alone having been a target of assaults from Mongols and Chinese and Portuguese long before the Tamils began attacking the temple said to contain it. Sri Lanka's two million Muslims felt menaced by both Hindus and Buddhists, while Marxists were currently being co-opted by the same forces that had killed them only a generation before. In 1959 a prime minister had been assassinated by a Buddhist priest.

At times, people hopefully assured me, Tamil kings had

protected Buddhism, and Sinhalese rulers had taken on Indian queens and advisers and texts; but many here still took pride in the local belief that the Buddha had come to the island three times and was said to have told a disciple, as he was dying, that the true home of his teachings was "Lanka." Nine of the seats in parliament now were held by monks, and they were among the most passionate advocates for violence. Before the recent elections, Tamil leaders had urged their people not to vote, so that the hard-line nation-alists would come to power—as they did—and there'd be a pretext for more fighting.

I'd been struck, on arrival, that the Sri Lankan flag was the only one I'd seen that featured a sword, brandished between the paws of a capering lion. Later, I'd learn that a group of monks had set up a political party whose em-blem showed the lion thrusting its sword forwards, on the offensive.

———

It was strange to come upon a Buddhist country that seemed to enshrine the notion of an earthly paradise: the Buddha himself had left his gilded home at the age of twenty-nine precisely in order to quit a walled garden and find a way of living with the harder truths of mortal existence. His first discourse, in Sarnath, was about curing unease within our-

selves, not seeking out some external heaven. Faced with the
demon Mara—as in the fresco I'd seen in the cave temples of
Dambulla—he'd sat untroubled, unwilling to yield to the
anger, greed or confusion that marks a true paradise lost. Yet
here in Sri Lanka, many Buddhists spoke of their country as
a chosen land, as if every land could not be chosen if seen in
the right light. The disquieting implication was that its residents could do anything they chose, since they were already
saved by their faith—while others could do whatever they
chose since they were condemned by their distance from it.

What made this all more agonizing was that Sri Lanka
really did enjoy many features of Arcadia. On the train
from Colombo to Kandy, I'd seen laughing girls walking
hand in hand through the green and golden light. Monks
were making their way under umbrellas along railway
tracks back to their temples. The signs beside them said
SPEED 5 M.P.H. After the many-headed clamor and congestion of India, the whole place seemed blessedly serene, as
untroubled as a statue of the Buddha. People were moving
with a gentle island sway; this might have been India in a
rocking chair, on a verandah above the sea.

It's so easy, I thought, to place paradise in the past or the
future—anywhere but here. In the hill station of Nuwara
Eliya, where homesick Brits had once remade a fog-bound
version of Wiltshire or Somerset, I found the walls of a shop
still advertising "Haberdashers, Ladies' Draperies, Travelling

Requisites, Aerated Water." In the musty Scottish-style hotel where I spent the night, permanently dank in the misty, almost drizzling afternoons, a whole bookcase was given over to ancient Penguin titles—*The Hero of Herat*, *No Kava for Johnny*, *Dead Man's Rock*—that cast a nostalgic glow over a long-lost age.

Here, I thought, was a place that had been called paradise so often by outsiders that it had been confirmed in the belief. The beauty of travel is that a visitor can see graces in a place that locals may take for granted; but here in Sri Lanka, I was ever more haunted by its shadow side: perhaps my very presence here enabled the island to affix a sticker of Paradise on top of more thorny truths.

In any case, each day when I went to breakfast and opened the local newspapers, reality came roaring back. On page 2, a grisly color photo of the shattered car in which the deputy chief of staff of the Sri Lankan Army had been assassinated by a suicide bomber, just down the road, my first morning in the country. Not far away, a report on the journalist who had been gunned down a few days later, three miles from where I was buttering my toast.

One of the national newspapers, as every morning, was urging its readers to write to the guerrilla leader to remind him that fighting wasn't kind or civil. Another ran the merry headline, "Let's Go Off to War!"

"Wishes are a risky business," muses the keen-eyed driver at the heart of Romesh Gunesekera's eerie set of stories about his native land, *Noontide Toll*. The narrator is surveying the Russian playboys flocking into the fantasy island for massages, the Germans hungry for "sun, samadhi and plush aromatherapy." As he guides foreigners around the trappings of a paradise restored, he holds his tongue about tour guides who are in fact off-duty soldiers, five-star guest-houses that were, until recently, bullet-riddled ghost houses. He notices a hotel manager whose trigger finger is "callused and discoloured at the edge." He registers bright-eyed hotel workers promising "climate control, rain-showers, triple X Adult TV," as if they'd never heard of the English rock star busted for pedophilia here. If children can be scarred for life by trauma, I thought, what shadows must haunt cultures that are being constantly reborn?

And what is it about these paradise places, I kept thinking, that throws off such a disquieting charge? Sri Lanka's longtime rival in Asia's fantasy-island stakes was Bali, and I often thought of the Hindu island tucked into largely Muslim Indonesia as I watched the village girls here bathing in streams, the boys, two to a saddle, bicycling down sunlit lanes. In both places, there was an uncommon sense that all borders between the spirit world and the human had been dissolved.

My wife, coming from a land of ghosts, Japan, couldn't sleep all the time we were in Bali. But she couldn't be sure she was awake, either. "Look," she whispered, turning away when we visited some art galleries, her first afternoon on the island. "You can't tell where the trees end and the humans begin." There were faces watching us even in our room, she felt; we were moving through a crowded world of witches and spells, where we couldn't read any of the signs or even tell light from dark.

Every home in Bali, the guidebooks assured us, contains a temple. But what that means in practice is that the visitor is entering a realm saturated with rites she can't begin to follow. When violence broke out across Indonesia in 1965, allegedly in response to a threat from communism, it reached terrible heights in Bali, where at least eighty thousand people were slaughtered in a matter of months, often by smiling neighbors bearing machetes. Some murderers were said to drink their victims' blood.

It was a feature of paradise that it observed laws that the outsider couldn't fathom. Any place of angels, as Bali initially seemed to be, has to contain its darker sides, too, not to mention serpents. Even in Eden peace proved temporary; the offspring of our "first parents" were a killer and his victim. The more I bumped around Sri Lanka, the more

I began to wonder whether real faith might have less to do with a conviction that everything will turn out all right than with the simple confidence that something makes sense, even when everything goes wrong.

———

As a monk, Thomas Merton knew that paradise inheres in no place, but only in the mind one brings to it. And when he took off for Asia, he was perhaps seeking to deepen his own faith by exposing himself to the beliefs of others; it had been a Hindu swami, after all, who had first urged him to read St. Augustine and *The Imitation of Christ*. For Merton, more than for many, faith was a never-ending work in progress; to keep his devotion alive, he seemed to need challenges and doubt at least as much as stability.

It was thrilling, as I sat in my room with the sea crashing outside, to read about how Sri Lanka had returned the searching monk to a kind of innocence. "Wow!" he'd written, as he'd seen Orion "hanging almost upside down" in the southern skies and tried to find the Southern Cross; I remembered how, each day, when I entered the Dalai Lama's hotel room after breakfast, I'd glimpsed a telescope pointed out the window towards the unfamiliar heavens. Merton had marveled at the flowers and the lushness all around, his first taste of the tropics. "Ceylon is incomparable!" he'd exclaimed at one moment: no naïf, but someone who saw that Paradise cannot be separated from difficulty or squalor. When Buddhists speak of a lotus in mud, they're reminding us that the most beautiful of flowers has its roots in what we regard as muck and filth; it's only grit that makes the radiance possible.

The talismanic word "Lanka" had first arrived in my life when I was two years old and my father came to my bedside every evening in our chill, gray flat in North Oxford and began reading me the foundational Hindu epic, the *Ramayana*. It tells of how Sita, the beautiful bride of the god Rama, is abducted by a demon king, who carries her off to an island fortress twenty-one miles across the water: "Lanka." The fallen angel who kidnaps her wins her trust by posing as an ascetic; he is the son of sages, and it's said he cannot be killed by either gods or spirits. Of course, I'd think later, every place likes to demonize its neighbor: if heaven is here, then hell must be that place across the water.

Yet it was my father, of Tamil descent, who came back from a trip to Sri Lanka telling me how sweet the people were, and how friendly and easygoing their lives seemed to be. Things felt so laid-back compared with India in those years before the war; in the tropical sun, many seemed to have not a care in the world. Paradise, too, is the place just across the border.

In the very heart of Sri Lanka sits a great forested out-cropping above the tea bushes with a depression at the top, which can be taken to be a giant footprint. Buddhists hold that this mark at the top of Adam's Peak was left by the Buddha himself, on his third trip to the island. Christians, however, sometimes ascribe the imprint to Jesus's disciple Thomas. Hindus have taken it to belong to Shiva, spinning creation and destruction into being with his dance. Muslims have been heard to suggest that it is the mark of Adam, who took his leave of Paradise, weeping, at this very spot.

But when I made the pilgrimage to the sacred peak, passing through one checkpoint after another to reach the 5,500 steps ascending to the summit, I could see little, this midsummer day, for the clouds. And the place that was home to the hopes of so many religious traditions was almost empty. A single cook remained in the Japanese peace pagoda, its lone monk having left for the season. A forestry commission official on hand seemed most eager to speak about the year he'd spent in that paradise known as Providence, in Rhode Island.

The main thing the holy site offered, in fact, was a lesson about our eagerness to project our hopes on what we do not know. Marco Polo, who had devoted half of the short passage he'd written on the island to the mountain, had never set foot on the island at all, I was now told. And the man who had given Adam's Peak its name—the British traveler and fabulist Sir John Mandeville—had never even existed, I heard upon returning to the capital.

I'd been rattled and unsettled by Sri Lanka as by no other place I could remember; the idea of paradise seemed to corrupt its real moments of beauty and to move people to be not kinder but more reckless. Yes, the guidebooks might blithely speak of how you could find Adam and Eve in the north, in their graves; they were less apt to mention that Marco Polo, in his few paragraphs, had claimed that Adam had died on the peak named after him, and the Buddha, too.

When I opened up Merton's *Asian Journal* again, back in the capital, I noticed how excited he'd been simply to board a plane in San Francisco, near a "silent Hawaiian soldier." The "moment of take-off was ecstatic." Watching the plane's windows as it "wept jagged shining courses of tears," he'd given voice to joy. "May I not come back," he wrote, "without having settled the great affair."

Above the blue Pacific, heading away from all the worlds he'd known, he'd felt, "I am going home, to the home where I have never been in this body." But what kind of home awaited him? Barely two months later, days after his transfiguration with the Buddhas, he was being flown back on a US Air Force plane, his dead body surrounded by the bodies of soldiers lost to the Vietnam War.

III

City of Tomorrow

Their ages when they died were twenty-four or twenty-three years or seventy-four days. They were described in the barely legible letters on the headstones as an infant daughter, a seventeen-year-old son. The names beside them were fragrant with homesickness: Epsom and Abingdon and Surrey. Each inscription seemed a poignant sequel to the buildings all around—Glendower and Ascot and St. Andrew's—and to the hot water bottles, the billiards tables, the fraying pages of P. G. Wodehouse with which the self-exiled had for so long tried to bring home a little closer.

Long after I left Sri Lanka, I was back there again in memory, in the one place of peace I'd found across the troubled island: the British Garrison Cemetery tucked away on a small unmarked ridge in the Buddhist capital of Kandy. In the realm of politics, people speak of "divide-and-rule,"

East and West, your God and mine; here I'd found something so human that such tags seemed a little beside the point.

"Man appoints but God can disappoint," I read on one worn gravestone. "We walk by faith, not by sight." The Buddhist town around the Christian sentences brought back to me the words of St. Paul: "In hope we are saved, but hope is not hope if its object is seen."

The ages on the headstones were shocking: six months, seven months, twenty-six years old. The causes of death were "cirrhosis of the liver" or warfare, constant accidents: "impaled while disembarking from a horse." Unexpected serpents. Beneath all the words, the deepest cause of all was probably foreignness itself.

They'd come so far to try to remake home in some more idyllic form. The headstones had been shipped over from Britain, on vessels that carried back cocoa and rubber and tea. Only a few minutes away were St. Paul's Church and the Queen's Hotel, not to mention the Temple of the Tooth. Merton had found the memorial tablets he'd seen across the island "curiously touching in their 'eloquence.'"

But it was sobering, too, to realize that the calmest place in the land was a city of the dead. Not just a reminder that oblivion exists even in a seeming paradise—"Et in Arcadia ego," as the paintings of the seventeenth century liked to show—but a reminder that all our ideas of how right we are will soon be leveled. No, I didn't believe that paradise was the exclusive province of the dead; but perhaps it could be apprehended only when we remembered that nothing—nothing—lasts.

> Can you see me, stranger, at your doorway
> Of a ruined house or standing where
> Your home once was, a mound of earth
> And later, nothing.

Jean Arasanayagam, who'd composed those lines, had written just down the road.

———

It had been a hot day in June after many hours of turmoil, when I'd leaned in to make out the writing on one of the headstones, barely legible after centuries of weather: "Died suddenly of sunstroke at Rozel Estate, Ambegoda." I sensed a movement among the trees beyond, and then a man who had been stretched out along a trunk, cradling a newspaper, stood up and came towards me.

I braced myself for a plaintive request or whisper of the kind I'd heard everywhere across the island; people seemed often to be emerging here from the trees. This man, however, spoke in a brisk English that dispelled many of my assumptions.

"I work here," he said, extending a hand. "Charles Carmichael."

Such a British name, to go with the tomato-bright shirt, the crisp gray hair neatly parted on one side, the gray trousers. Sri Lanka is as rich as southern India in Johns and Thomases and Abrahams, as well as de Souzas and Fonsecas and Fernandezes, names recalling couplings or conversions from centuries before. This Carmichael, however, was very dark, and his name did not suggest Portuguese Catholics or missionary hopes. He spoke my language with an ease and authority I hadn't met often across his land.

"I come from an English-language household," he explained, as if he saw the question that was coming. His grandfather, he went on—a good, upstanding Carmichael—had visited a Hindu priest here and found himself quite taken with the holy man's daughter. She was only fifteen, but the British were in charge and they could claim any prize they wanted. Very soon, the girl was big with Carmichael's child, and the man was taking off, alone, for Calcutta.

This stranger wasn't entirely without conscience, however, his grandson assured me. Unusually for the times, he sent back money for his—well, for his child's mother—and for the boy's education. Another Englishman had later come upon the young, unattended mother and made her pregnant a few more times.

Perhaps Charles saw in my English voice and Indian features someone else not keen to deal in simple either-ors; he told me that the British had left only gravestones in exchange for all they'd carried home. But he also stressed that they had brought blessings, here and there. Things were shoddy in Sri Lanka, he admitted, and not only because of the war; sometimes people missed the solidity, the discipline of the Brits.

"Most of these graves have been torn up," he volunteered, a little as a host might apologize to a guest who's surprised him while cleaning. "By looters, people looking for treasure. They thought there would be jewels here, family heirlooms. They didn't know the English don't take their treasures to their graves. So now we're in a state of terrible neglect."

That was why he had been appointed to come and make a good show of everything in advance of Prince Charles's visit, some years before.

"And after the visit, they asked me to stay on, to keep it intact."

I looked across the stunted grass, the stones with their faded names.

"Do many English people come here to find their roots?"

"Oh, yes. I've been working in this place eight years. There have been seven visitors."

"Seven in eight years?"

"They're getting old. It's hard to climb the hill to get here."

"Now"—he perked up, not wanting to lose his eighth—"you see that grave over there? 'Died of sunstroke at Rozel Estate.' Well, Rozel Estate is not very hot. What happened is that he ran into a wild elephant. The elephant must have chased him, and so he must have got very warm, and fainted of sunstroke."

Nearby lay a governor's wife, the victim of diarrhea, Charles explained; the headstone was obliged to dress up the unlovely truth. Another man, he pointed out, had died "from the falling of a house."

"Sabot-age," said my kindly guide, his stress on the "age," reminding me that he'd never seen the country from which his words flowed so fluently. "The English do things properly. Their houses don't fall down like ours."

In the distance, a tall memorial recalled a man who had once been the most powerful in the area. Upon his death, Charles told me, the man had left his money not to his own children, but to all the children in Sri Lanka who were—"what is the word, 'il-legitimate'? Who had English fathers and Sinhalese mothers. Because he knew their lives would be difficult."

He paused. "It's so unusual, that kind of selflessness."

———

I'd long been drawn to graveyards in the places where cultures cross if only because headstones put every kind of division in its place. I recalled Lord Elgin, the viceroy, sleeping forever in a grave outside the neglected Anglican church down the road from the Dalai Lama's home in northern India, where a local priest played a cassette of Cat Stevens's "Morning Has Broken" on Easter Sunday. In southern Yemen I'd met a stranger strikingly similar to Charles—he had English blood, though he looked very much of the East—who'd led me around the headstones in Aden's Christian Cemetery, the only thing in town worth seeing, he said, of a place where nobody lived far from death.

In Kashmir, when I'd inadvertently asked poor Jonny if we could step through the green door that was usually locked, we'd come upon a riot of overgrown weeds, whose fresh white crosses all bore Indian names. But farther in, where few would venture, we read of a Lavinia, a "Mabel Emily, a Darling Wife," even Robert Thorpe, the British officer who'd urged his superiors to send medical help to Kashmir and died, perhaps a victim of his support for Kashmiri independence, at the age of thirty.

This was a nominally segregated place—reserved for Christians, mostly British—yet it was the one space on the island where I wasn't being reminded of chosen people and unchosen, conqueror and conquered. The most human of communities, it was the least divided. When Melville had wandered around Jerusalem—"a city besieged by army of the dead"—he, too, had noticed how, in death, Greek and Roman and Armenian finally all slept together.

One headstone here had been erected by "sorrowing friends in remembrance of [a friend's] amiability and wisdom." Another, Mr. Carmichael told me, belonged to a "traitor," an Englishman who, seeing Sinhalese approach, had deserted his post and fled. There was a scholar here, famous for his command of Sanskrit and Pali, a man who had fought against Napoleon and, having survived four wars, had finally met his end in Sri Lanka. There was the grave of a man who had traveled along the river to chronicle the country's villages, and contracted a disease and been forced to abandon the project. Simply getting to know the country could prove fatal.

Killed by falling trees, killed by falling houses; Elliot, Fenerson, Freckletown, Garnock. From Lewes, Aberdeenshire, Weraloo. Whole lives compressed into a few words or lines. The most recent body had arrived in 1951, that of a woman who had been denied entrance in the early days of independence until the church pursued action against the local council and set her where she belonged.

Few of them had probably seen what was coming: our

lives can only be half known insofar as their final act, which seems to put all that has come before in place, is always hidden, and we seldom wish to think of it. We step out of the play with no chance to think back on it—and even as we're trying to make sense of life, things are shifting, falling away from us on every side. The older I got, the more I began to feel that almost everything that had happened to me, good or bad, seemed to have come out of nowhere. As Leonard Cohen, faithful for life to the Old Testament, put it in one of his final songs, we're "none of us deserving the cruelty or the grace."

———

What must it be like, I wondered as I followed Charles around, to spend your waking life among the dead? How would it shadow your thoughts, give fleshly life to your notions of the afterworld? In his novel *Mardi*, Melville's narrator describes coming upon an idyllic island on which not a single gravestone is to be seen. Only later does he realize that's because the locals carry their dead out to sea. Soon, the constant hiss and surge of the waves come to sound to him like the cries of the departed.

In Japan a cemetery is known as a "city of tomorrow." And this Christian cemetery in Sri Lanka's Buddhist capital was in the hands of a man who had many cultures inside him, much like the Kandyan poet Arasanayagam. He'd never suffered from his mixed inheritance, Charles now assured me, though he had been denied a passport because he did not have three generations of ancestors born on the faraway island.

Had I spoken to Charles on the phone, I might have seen someone blond, tall, from a goodish school, perhaps, the kind of upright fellow played by Charles Dance in the movies. Had I read about this place, or seen it online, I might have reached for whatever the fashionable conclusions of the moment were. Good riddance on oppressors, or "those were the days." But here in the hot sun, standing with this loyal caretaker, both of us in some ways the product of the meetings between cultures, we were in the company of more complex feelings.

Once upon a time, when the other Charles, from Buckingham Palace, was due to visit, the Tamils had launched an attack on the Temple of the Tooth nearby, and the prince's security officers had told him it wasn't safe to stop by. So he flew over the site in a helicopter.

"They were wise to keep him from coming," Charles Carmichael went on. "The Tamils have been so clever at assassinating everyone they choose. Our own soldiers, too; they are careless. Not like the British. Quite capable of shooting someone by mistake."

He led me into his little office, where a book written

many years before had teased out the stories that now he was sharing with his visitor. On one wall was a tiny framed letter from Prince Charles, elegantly assuring his hosts how sorry he was to have missed the opportunity to see the graveyard. I hope one day, said the heir to the crown, to be able to see the really interesting places in Sri Lanka. The other Charles was patiently awaiting him in what had the feeling of a never-ending tomorrow.

Afterworld

The minute I stepped out of the clanking, near-empty cable car, I was in another world. An empty parking lot in front of me, a narrow unmarked road beyond. Not much of anything else: visitors were not permitted to walk from here into town and for more than a millennium, until around 1872, no woman had even been allowed to set foot here. Five minutes below me, at the base of the mountain, was Gokurabashi, or the "Bridge of Heaven."

It was hard to believe that, only ninety minutes earlier, I'd been in the noisy heart of crowded Osaka, screens flashing, bodies surging, a woman in a suit propping her iPad next to her McFlurry. Now I was twenty-eight hundred feet above sea level, a train having carried me through fifty-one ever more ghostly stations to the end of the line, the Bridge of Heaven.

Finally, a country bus appeared and bore me around a

series of switchback turns. Little to see here but trees, a yellow sign announcing the imminence of bears. As we drew towards the center of the settlement, the cypress-bark roofs of 117 temples, like the prows of seagoing vessels about to sail off into the mist.

I shivered when I got out of the bus. Not just because the air was twenty degrees cooler on the Fahrenheit scale than in the cities of the plain. More because there was such an accumulated stillness to the place. A thin path ran like a nave past a row of temples to another bridge, where the faithful wash their hands and face before entering the most solemn "city of tomorrow" in the land: a graveyard containing two hundred thousand souls, in a forest of high cedars, many of them here for three hundred years or longer.

I made my slow way down the unpeopled street, as if through a still life. Everyone who stays on the mountain has to sleep in a temple; every visitor has, for the duration of her stay, to live like a monk. At last I came to the fourteenth-century temple where a room awaited me and passed between high, thick wooden gates to heavy doors that had been pulled open.

"Hello?" I called, and an elderly monk appeared before me.

I gave him my name, and he checked it off on a print-out. "Dinner, five thirty," he barked in telegraphic English. "No onion, no garlic, no meat, no fish. Breakfast seven o'clock. One hour before, goma ceremony. Door close, eight o'clock."

I stepped up to take off my shoes and heard him roar, "Wrong!" I was sloughing them off one step too high.

Giving up one's preferences, I gathered, was the first step towards liberation.

———

After I'd dropped my bags off in a bare tatami room, I washed my hands in a long communal basin. The water stung, it was so cold. Back out in the street, I saw figures dressed in white, the traditional color of a shroud; they were carrying begging bowls and wearing conical hats above the shawls that stood for Buddhist robes. The holy mountain Koyasan marks the end point of three separate pilgrimages, though most of the people I could see were followers of the Shingon order of Buddhism. Having made a ritual circumnavigation of eighty-eight temples on the island of Shikoku, they now had arrived at the climax of their trip, their Pure Land, or Paradise.

Ten million such devotees live across Japan, but the details of their mystical order are so secret that, it's said, they weren't written down, even in Japanese, for a thousand years. For all that time, few outsiders were allowed to set foot on the mountain, which once had been home to fifteen hundred monasteries. When the mother of the monk who founded the monastic complex attempted the thirteen-mile ascent to her son's domain, she was rebuffed, so it's believed, by a thunderstorm.

By now it was getting dark—hard to imagine I'd been in sunlit Sri Lanka ten weeks earlier—and I returned to my empty room for twelve lacquer bowls filled with sesame tofu, mountain vegetables, sweet-and-sour seaweed in vinegar. After nightfall, when I ventured out again, only a few pilgrims were visible, halting at sacred sites along the road to chant—as if on some Buddhist Via Dolorosa—while a leader clacked a bowl and shook what sounded like bells. At the end of the road was the bridge where they would perform their ablutions and enter, effectively, the province of the dead.

I walked up to the sacred crossing-place and saw a long trail of stone lanterns disappearing between the dwarfing trees. Follow that path for a mile, I'd read, and I would come to the mausoleum of Kobo Daishi, the man who'd created the order and its monasteries, believed to be sitting still in meditation 1,171 years after he stopped breathing. Little else was apparent in the settlement of barely four thousand.

There are two celebrated gateways to paradise, I remembered reading in a compendious anthology of descriptions of such worlds, *The Book of Heaven*. One hinges on vision, the other on death.

———

In the two-room apartment that we rent in the land of the living—a Western-style flat in a modern suburb, three hours north of the holy mountain—my Japanese wife maintains a household altar in one corner of our living room. Every morning, in front of framed photos of her dead mother and dead father, she lays out fresh food and green tea for her parents and begins to chant, at very high speed. On her days off from work, she steps onto a bus for a two-hour trip, via three trains, to their graves, to bring them up to date on all that's happening in the family. When I asked her recently why she'd begun reading so much, she reminded me that now her book-loving mother was gone, she was obliged to devour novels on behalf of her parent in the afterworld.

I thought of this when I started walking around Koyasan, which has the feeling of a home for departed spirits in one corner of Japan. The doors between the living and the dead are kept open across the land, and at intervals throughout the year lanterns are lit so the dead can make their way back to earth and look in on their much-missed loved ones. Divisions between animate and inanimate are porous here, and our future homes, in the afterworld, are within earshot, it's believed, of our present ones. Koyasan sits near the geographic center of the nation, tucked within a ring of eight outer and eight inner mountains, which cradle it like a hidden treasure within a set of lotus petals. When I'd located an English-language website for one of its temples, I'd read, "There is a heaven far to the westward of this world."

The ancestral and the sacred were one, in short, though in a different way from Aboriginal Australia; the pilgrims all around were praying not just for the departed but to them. For my Japanese neighbors, those who die are believed to become Buddhas and grow closer to us in death, often, than they were in life. Such intimacy could apply even to the local hero named Kukai, who, at the age of thirty, in the year 804, sailed for T'ang dynasty China to plumb the mysteries of what is called Tantric Buddhism and brought them back to Japan under the name "Shingon," or "True Word."

He had come to this particular mountain, it was said, when, after his return, he'd awoken from a meditative trance to see a hunter, accompanied by a black dog and a white dog. This mysterious band led him up to a site where no human tracks could be seen. It seemed a perfect setting for the esoteric Buddhism he'd mastered in just eight months in China. Initiates of Shingon deploy mudras, or hand gestures, as in Tibet, and recite mantras, or hypnotic chants, that bring them closer, it's said, to the secret rhythm of the universe; they hold, as only a few do even in Tibet, that if you master various ascetic practices, you can attain enlightenment in a single lifetime. Indeed, it was an object shaped like a thunderbolt—symbol of the Vajrayana Buddhism known in many parts of Tibet—that Kukai had flung from a beach in China before his departure and, so it was said, discovered again on the mountain here, as by a miracle.

In the years to come, I'd find myself visiting this holy mountain more than once with the Dalai Lama; the monks who accompanied him would tell me that the unrelenting Japanese fare was not always easy for them, but the grave silence and darkness were ideal for meditation. "Death is part of our life," I heard the Tibetan leader say, one morning of thick mist and heavy silence, the maples rusting all around. "So long as you understand that, it won't be a shock."

For now, I was surrounded by mostly elderly Japanese, bowing and chanting as they walked from one shrine to the next in white shirts whose backs read "We Devote Our Lives to Kobo Daishi." Such devotion seemed in part to involve sitting as if lifeless amid the graves. Eighty-six years after Kukai appeared to expire—one month after he'd built the first temple on the mountain, in 835—an emperor bestowed on him the honorific title "Kobo Daishi," or "Great Master Who Spread the Buddhist Teaching." For those who follow him, death means simply a journey to an adjoining room; every morning monks in saffron robes bear a blond-wood box on a palanquin between the trees, to offer the long-meditating saint fresh food for breakfast, then for lunch.

I'd always felt at home in monasteries; sometimes I thought the austerities and strict obediences of my school in England had been a training in living simply in a cell, focused on something deeper than our résumés. When I'd left New York City, five months before I turned thirty, it had been to live in a temple in Kyoto. Here, though, there was none of the bustle and collegial warmth I'd come to know in the Benedictine monastery where I stay four times a year; Koyasan felt less like an arrow released through the air than one held back in preparation, all contained intensity.

The sound of a gong, reverberating along the corridors, awoke me my first morning in the temple. I could hear chants in the distance, and as I tiptoed along the creaking wooden floors, I smelled incense, and came upon monks in rows in a prayer hall in the predawn dark, enacting their daily fire ceremony. Every day they burned 108 pieces of wood, as if to purge their illusions; every day they scattered 108 sesame seeds, as if to bring the Buddha into their beings.

"The whole of life here is sometimes like a drawing," said a Swiss monk who introduced himself as Kurt, when I stepped into a funky café on the main street after a morning of walking through the treasure halls of temples. "Everything is a mandala. This is all paradise." The minute he'd set foot on the mountain, twenty-seven years before, he'd known that he'd come home. He'd been living at Muryokoin, the Temple of Immeasurable Light, around the corner, for nine years.

"When you think of a mountain in Europe," Kurt went on, "what do you see? Blue skies, sunshine, space. Here in Japan mountains are dark. In Europe people talk of mountains as 'ladders to heaven.' Here in Japan, people come to the mountains in order to die."

Fire as purgation, in short, not as destruction; fire as a way of releasing us from attachments, even from our simple sense of what is right. I couldn't help feeling I'd arrived in a kind of bardo, the half known realm that encircles those who have left the land of the living and are waiting to be directed to their next home.

———

By a curious kind of intuition, the book I'd brought to read on the quiet mountain was a collection of Emily Dickinson's poems; perhaps I sensed that she might be the perfect accompaniment to a world of temples, having spent twenty-six years without leaving her house, entertaining Death and Premonition and Eternity and Light in her small room. She'd "died before she died," as the mystics say; by staying within her cell, she'd traveled to the farthest reaches of doubt and conviction, seeing how "we both believe, and disbelieve a hundred times an hour."

Not far from her room, Emerson and Thoreau were finding a kind of homemade paradise where they sat; but Dickinson, like her unsettled contemporary Melville, sustained a keen sense of all that could never be fathomed. Much of the time she seemed to be keeping company with what she couldn't see through; she treated what she didn't know with intimacy, as if it were her daily familiar.

Whenever I lost myself in Dickinson's poems of passion and illumination—even of terror—I never came away feeling hers was a partial or unsatisfied life. In many ways it seemed richer, fuller than those of her contemporaries who lived in the everyday world. Such paradise as she found, she found only within a cloud of unknowing.

We humans, William James would write decades later, are akin to dogs in a library: we're surrounded by extraordinary wisdom and knowledge, but entirely in a form we cannot decipher. All we can do is give ourselves over to what we cannot know. I turned a page in Dickinson and read: "Wonder is not precisely knowing and not precisely knowing not."

———

Next day, I took the long walk all the way to the Okunoin, or "innermost sanctum," at the end of the path between the cedars. It was, inevitably, a walk through Japan's history books, since emperors and shoguns and such central leaders as Hideyoshi Toyotomi are buried here; but in their midst are Chinese Christians, Kabuki actors, common soldiers. It was bracing again to witness the companionship of the dead, to be reminded of how little we could ever glean of what Hamlet called "the undiscovered country, from whose bourn no traveler returns."

It was humbling, too, and even more than in the cemetery in Sri Lanka, to recognize how much the arguments of theology are beside the point. Even in this place of religious intensity, the Dalai Lama, when I heard him speak, tried to nudge lay listeners away from religion (and its certainties) towards what he habitually called "common experience and common sense and scientific findings." It made me think that paradise, by definition, has to be available to all of us, though not, I hoped, only in the grave.

Kobo Daishi, I now learned, had edited a dictionary, had introduced the use of coal to his nation, had called upon the secret texts he'd mastered to end a drought. But even more essential was that he had united the Buddhism he'd mastered with the indigenous Japanese animist folk-tradition of Shinto, so that the ancient spirits of rivers and mountains seemed to protect the arriving forms of Buddhism. For all its cathedral quiet, the cemetery felt crowded as I walked among the graves. This was partly due, no doubt, to the Japanese Buddhist belief that the dead never really leave the world; but it was surely deepened by the Shinto notion that every last blade of grass and speck of dust has a soul. "We even include hell in our mandalas of enlightenment," the Swiss monk Kurt had assured me.

Most monks in Japan are pressed into robes because of family obligations: a father dies and, overnight, his office-worker son has to drop the life he knows and undergo years of punishing training to take up an ancestral place in a temple. One night, as I wandered around the graveyard, I found myself walking in step with a fresh-faced monk in his midthirties who told me how, just two years earlier, he'd been performing a white-collar job in central Osaka, heading to his office every morning like any other salaryman.

Now his office was the cemetery, and he tended to the dead as once he might have to his accounts. We walked past the mascot of a well-known pantyhose company above one tomb and a great marble slab put up by the Sharp company, on which, I was told, I could see my reflection as I passed, as on a high-definition TV screen. Enlightenment, the monk didn't need to say, means seeing the light in everything—even that grave shaped like a rocket ship.

Every morning, when I awoke, I started now to go to fire ceremonies in various temples; one of them had constructed a whole structure above the main street, in which a kind of bonfire blazed at 7:00 a.m. every day. I thought, as I sat beside it, of the afternoon when I'd been caught for three hours in the worst fire in California history at the time, sitting on a mountain road and watching the flames above take apart our living room, reduce every keepsake in my bedroom to ash, wipe out every trace of the bright future I had planned, laid out in my scribbled pages. A devastation at the time, it seemed. But when I began to help my mother draft a plan for a new house, I realized I was free to construct a new life closer to the one I'd always wanted.

Maybe, I thought, the point of Koyasan was to help one see every fleeting object and event as part of some hidden design, just as the Swiss monk had suggested. Maybe in a world reduced to essentials, a single blade of grass could be seen as a world of flame. This might not be consoling but it was part of the monk's practice: to savor what he saw and live calmly with what he could not know.

Not long thereafter I dragged Hiroko up to the holy mountain, so we could partake together of its mysteries. As we walked around the garden in our temple, we noticed that a little shrine containing offerings and symbols had been vandalized; some wild animal must have ransacked the site where offerings are left out for the gods.

That night, I awoke in the dark and, looking across the room, saw Hiroko standing in the blackness. I let out a scream—her face looked wraith-pale—and she, terrified at my outburst, screamed as well.

Afterwards, neither of us could sleep again, though we'd been routinely passing each other in the night for more than twenty years.

———

Hiroko had long maintained, as people around the Himalayas do, that mountains are particular homes to gods, and in Japan it was easy to credit the belief. The streets of the modern country were rebuilt after the war along a Western model, extended to the nth degree; they're a jangle of amusement arcades, 7-Elevens, gas stations stretching out towards the rice paddies. The urban mess of the Far West can seem orderly and quiet by comparison. Yet every time I drove up from Kyoto to Mount Hiei, barely ten minutes away, I was back in a place that felt deeply unchanged. There was snow on the ground often, not a figure visible; bells tolled between the trees, and almost nothing I could see told me which century I was in.

One day on Koyasan I asked the Swiss monk Kurt which season was the best time to visit, and he almost spat out his coffee at the naivete, the insolence of my question.

"Can you say the trees are not beautiful when they are bare?" he all but shouted. "I have taken photographs when the snow is in the temples. Big wedges of it, but so soft. And through the snow you can see a thousand little points of light. And then in the spring, there are cherry blossoms, and then rhododendron . . ."

By the time he'd taken me through the beauties of every season, I'd been reminded that joy, for a monk, is never the same as pleasure, because it has nothing to do with changing circumstance.

———

And so my days on the mountain went on, and started to intensify, and I began to fall into a kind of rhythm, as if awakening to a state of clarity in which empty rooms could seem full and no detail was ever entirely profane. At times, it's true, I wondered if I'd stumbled into a Kobo Daishi Divinity Center, a sort of Shingon North Korea. The founder of the mountain was said to have established the first public school in the country, and to have created the hiragana script that offers a simplified and readable Japanese version of complicated Chinese characters. He was said to have discovered hot springs, to have been a calligrapher, a healer. "Kobo Daishi was also a civil engineer," a kindly local woman assured me, as if reciting from a textbook. "He invented a system for an irrigation pond. He was also a geologist—he found mercury."

Yet whenever the cult of personality began to feel too intense—even the magnolia was said to resemble the infant Kobo Daishi, seated amid lotus petals—I looked up to see monks go through annihilating routines in which no short-cuts were possible: bathing in a freezing river, visualizing the Buddha so intensely that they could become a Buddha themselves, chanting through the night. A Buddhist paradise has to be different from a Christian one—I watched twelve shaven-headed men in black stream out of a temple to go sit on a dark hill lit by candles—insofar as "in Buddhism, Cre-ator is ourself," as I'd heard the Dalai Lama put it.

Koyasan is a vespers place, I'd come to see; even at mid-day it has something of the stillness and gathering chill of late afternoon. And even in early autumn, I could feel the presence of the gold-and-black world I'd seen in photo-graphs of the long winter: great wooden buildings like slashes of bold calligraphy against thick snow. In the con-text of a chirpy, service-oriented society that has machines at every entrance calling out a welcome when there aren't humans to do so, Koyasan had the clarifying strictness of a nonnegotiable "Keep Out!"

By now, I was finding my way every night to the grave-yard, taking the long walk out to the mausoleums at the far end. Each time, when I walked across the first bridge, I felt the world of causality fall away. No thought of monk-or-layman now, no thought of living-or-dead. When I came to the final crossing, the "Bridge of Ignorance," as it is for the faithful, I entered what the devout regard as a world of illumination. Two lights in the Hall of Lanterns are said to have been burning for almost a thousand years; in one underground chamber, fifty thousand tiny statues of Kobo Daishi are lined up in long rows, shelf after shelf.

"When you are living in a world of typhoon, of fire and lightning," Kurt had told me—Koyasan has been assaulted at least four times by major fires—"you are living in the second. You don't wait for anything; you go out and use the day right now."

Paradise, in short, is regained by finding the wonder within the moment. As I walked among the farthest graves, I could hear the scuffling of small animals in the dark, the sudden hiss of a fluorescent light above the line of stone lanterns as it gave out, the last of the season's crickets. In one place the reflection from two lamps conferred golden eyes on a small stone statue.

Arriving at the mausoleum, I saw a man standing by himself, in the dim light of a few candles, shouting out the unearthly syllables of the Heart Sutra—"No eyes, no ears, no nose, no tongue, no body, no mind . . ." A prayer that could sound like a protection; it was lines from that text Hiroko had recited when, in a cave in Laos, she worried that my spirit was being taken away by some tall and enigmatic Buddhist statues.

I stepped back into the darkness to give him space, and then I saw a movement: a small, raccoon-faced creature foraging among pebbles for some food. A tanuki, I realized, the almost legendary badger-dog who is more often seen in stories than in real life. He looked at me intently, and continued with his scrabbling.

The next day I awoke at first light, splashed some water on my face from the rough communal basin and walked into a shadowy prayer hall where monks had gathered in the near-dark, barely lit by occasional tapers, while in an adjoining room a figure sat stock-still for half an hour, then began building a fire in the small wooden space.

In this vision of an afterlife, the fact of things passing was not a cause for grief so much as a summons to attention. All the light or beauty we could find, we had to find right now. The fact that nothing lasts is the reason why everything matters. If this was Shingon heaven, it meant that I had to take something of its undistracted clarity back to the fluorescent excitement of the in-between world in which I was dwelling, fifty-one stations away.

The thought that we must die, I might have heard the two hundred thousand graves saying, is the reason we must live well.

The Flames of Heaven

There were fires, six, seven of them, rising through the winter fog. Groups of men, scarves wrapped around their heads, eyes blazing in the half-light, were gathered, barefoot, around the flames, edging closer. A nearly naked figure with dusty, matted dreadlocks down to his waist was poking at a charred head with a bamboo pole. There was chanting in the distance, a shaking of bells, a furious drumming far away, and in the infernal no-light of the New Year dusk, I could make out almost nothing but orange blazes, far off, by the river.

How much of this was I dreaming? How much was I under a "foreign influence," if only of jet lag and displacement? Figures came towards me out of the mist, smeared in ash from head to toe, bearing the three-pronged spear of the holy city's patron, Shiva, "Ender of Time." I passed into a little alleyway behind the flames and arrived at a warren of tiny streets, in which a shrunken candle burned in the dark of a bare earth cavern. A boy was seated on the ground, behind a pair of scales. Cows were padding ceaselessly down the clogged, dung-splattered lane. Every now and then, another group of chanters surged past, a dead body under a golden shroud on the bamboo stretcher that they carried towards the river. I pressed myself against a wall, and a whisper of mortality brushed me.

I fumbled my way through the haze, in the labyrinth of narrow passageways, and another corpse came by, two women in their finest silk saris sludging barefoot through soft mud towards the holy waters. I followed intuition in and out of the dark streets, past little candles flickering in shrines and openings where men were whispering sacred syllables. Then, turning a corner, I came to an intersection and three men stood before me, guns protruding from behind their backs.

It was strange to think that, just seventy-two hours earlier, I had been on the far side of the world, marking a quiet New Year's Day in the sun. Now there were goats with auspicious red marks on their foreheads trotting around, and embers burning, and oil lamps drifting across the river in the fog. Along the walls were painted orange faces, laughing monkey gods, sacred looming phalluses. Shops on every side were selling sandalwood paste, and clarified butter for dead bodies, tiny clay urns for ashes.

The city of death had once been known as "Kashi," or "City of Light." The English writer Richard Lannoy, who all but lost his soul to Varanasi, had called it a "city of darkness and dream." In a long and often hallucinatory book, he had quoted the chief superintendent of police of what once was called Benares describing "the abduction of women from temples, prostitution in the name of God, the prevalence of theft on the pilgrim scene, the cannibalistic customs of the Aghoris [or extreme renunciates], the drunken orgies of bogus tantriks."

Yet what startled me most as I began to walk its streets was that the city of extinction was, without question, a city of joy. The people hurrying past me towards the burning pyres, bearing dead bodies towards the sacred river, were raising their voices in praise, and in a great, overwhelming cry of thanks.

———

I was heading, later that month, back to Sri Lanka, whose silent Buddhas surrounded by agitated locals had already denied me easy satisfactions, and also to Mauritius, another idyll where paradise villas are encircled by violence and terrible poverty. It seemed essential, in some way I couldn't explain, even to myself, to stop off, en route, at a city known as a crossing-ground, a place for moving from one dimension to another. Though Varanasi is said to be one of the oldest continuously inhabited cities on earth—as old as Xian or Thebes, claim the guidebooks—it had never been a center of political power; it had existed for more than two thousand years as a place of pilgrimage and a casting-off place for the life beyond. Bathe yourself in its filthy waters, devout Hindus believe, and you purify yourself for life. Die or be burned along its riverbanks, and you achieve moksha, or liberation from the cycle of incarnation.

Everything here acquired a different value. The heart of the city is a chaotic four-mile stretch of waterfront along the sacred river on which there are more than seventy ghats, or steps, from which the faithful can walk down into the water. At the top of these stand huge, many-windowed palaces and temples that are generally in a state of such advanced decay that they seem to speak for the impermanence of just about everything. At this very spot, the southeast-flowing Ganges turns around, for a short stretch, so it seems to be flowing back towards the Himalayas from which it came; bathers on its western bank face the rising sun.

Having never lived in India, having never observed the sacred-thread rites or Sanskrit incantations of Hinduism—I'd even begun to eat meat as soon as I entered boarding school—I looked on the pinwheeling rites around me as a tourist might. Or, perhaps worse, I looked on them as I might a coat a grandfather had passed down that didn't seem quite to fit. I didn't in truth come to Varanasi with the open eyes of a typical visitor from afar; as someone born to Hinduism, I assumed that I'd seen through the place already. The one attraction Varanasi held for me was that I was unlikely to mistake it for paradise.

Yet Varanasi transfixed me as only a cataclysm can. "See there, sir," cried a little boy, my first morning along the river. "Dead body is there!" As he started to recite his catechism—"Now, very strong chant, three hours to burn. Every body need two hundred kilos, wood. Everywhere, sir, dead body materials are there: flower, silk, clay pot, everything"—I began to understand why so many, whether they believe in gods or not, had been drawn here if only to work out what might be possible. "Heaven!" the boy cried in the infernal half-light. "Here everybody, he goes to heaven!"

The dirt on every side seemed itself a kind of admonition if only because it upended the logic of the everyday, inducting one into a different kind of calculus. The holy river in Varanasi flows past thirty sewers, with the result that the brownish water in which the devout bathe—many were drinking from it—contains three thousand times the maximum level of fecal coliform bacteria deemed safe for drinking by the World Health Organization. This was the city's first lesson for me: the holiest place in the land was also the filthiest. The near-fatal water could be turned, by devotion, into wine.

———————

The minute I'd stepped off the plane in Varanasi, fifty minutes after taking off from Delhi, I was lost in a purgatorial fog. I could barely see a few feet ahead of me. As I made my way across the tarmac towards the airport terminal, I saw a small figure with white hair shuffling through the mist ahead of me: Rosette, I realized, a ninety-one-year-old Parisienne I'd last seen attending teachings by the Dalai Lama in Dharamsala. By her side—it seemed the most natural thing in the world—was a Tibetan incarnate lama in his late eighties, now resident in New York, and an American monk in Tibetan red robes I'd bumped into most recently hurrying along Fifth Avenue.

Outside the front entrance to the terminal stood a great crowd of men in skullcaps, accompanied by women in black veils: pilgrims on their way to Mecca, I learned, being seen off by their loved ones. There were fourteen hundred mosques and other shrines here at the center of Hinduism. Conflicts between the religions had led to soldiers constantly on patrol, but that was never the city's central story. Then I stepped into a taxi, and was caught up in the swirling river of life that is at once Varanasi's central symbol and its feverish reality.

Urban India everywhere is an immersion in intensity—shock therapy of a kind—but the holy city inhabits a category all its own. The traffic was converging on every inch of road from every direction, yet, true to its mystic's contempt for reason, the place possessed no traffic lights. Here and there an elderly policeman with a mask over his mouth extended a hopeful arm, as cars, cows, bicycles, trucks heedlessly crashed past him. Dogs were sleeping in the middle of the busy road—Varanasi's Fifth Avenue, I surmised—and men were outstretched (sleeping, I hoped) along the side and on the pavement. A crowd had gathered in the middle of the street around a man who was dervishing around, whirling swords.

I knew the sacred waters had to be my first stop, so I dropped my bags off at a hotel and jumped into a car to head towards the ghats. In the course of the twenty-minute ride, we passed two jubilant corpse processions, two parades of children.

"This is a very inauspicious time," a young local turned round from the front seat to warn me (behind him I could see only a mass of raging, but unadvancing, bodies and vehicles, riding their horns). "It is called Kharmas. Everyone stays hidden in this time; no one talks about weddings, things like that. Everyone is silent. It is like a curse placed on the city."

If this was Varanasi at its most silent, I thought, almost unable to hear him as a train, too, thundered past on a brick bridge above us, I couldn't imagine it on one of its frequent festival days. "The curse lifts on January fourteenth," my new friend told me. "Then we celebrate." This was not cause for celebration for someone due, as I was, to leave on January thirteenth.

We got out at a Christian church and joined the crush of bodies pushing towards the holy river. The signs along the road spoke of "The Oldest Centre for Abacus Classes" and "Glorious Ladies Tailors," leaving me to wonder whether the glory lay with the ladies or their stitching. "British School for Languages is now Trounce Education," I read on another, offering a droll summary of the end of Empire. In Varanasi, half a million people are squeezed into the one-square-mile darkness of alleyways known as the Old City, with the result that some foreign visitors more or less give out, while others wonder if they've been slipped a tab of some foreign substance.

"Everything is always changing here," announced my guide as we arrived at the riverbank, where holy men were seated under colored umbrellas on the ground, chanting and smearing paste and ash on foreheads. "Different colors. Different spirit. Different energy. You have to be on high alert when you come to my city."

That much I'd gathered already.

We started walking along the river, dodging refuse and excrement on every side, and passed an almost naked man, staring at us, sheltered by a small fire inside a hut.

"He is meditating?" I tried.

"Everything for him is ashes," came the reply. "For these sadhus, they like very much to live with cremation. They don't wear clothes as we do. They don't do anything like people who are living in the material world. They want to live in a world of ash."

A little farther down, we almost walked into a man in a bright blue tunic and turban who was offering what seemed to be bon mots, as at a regular neighborhood barbershop (though here in Varanasi, the neighborhood barbershop, like the graveyard, the church and the zoo, was out on the street, and open to all). "Laughing Yogi," my guide explained, and broke into guffaws himself, as if abruptly propelled towards a sudden enlightenment.

A huge bloated cow floated slowly past. We clambered unsteadily into a small rocking boat, as, onshore, a handful of handsome young boys in elaborate gold pantaloons held up five-armed oil lamps and began practicing the purgation by fire they'd ritually perform that night. Other vessels were carrying pilgrims off to the dim other shore, a long, empty sandbank, so far as I could tell. Fires were blazing to north and to south, and the air was thick with the smell of incense and coal fires.

"Only this city, sir, you see twenty-four-hour cremation," offered the boatman, as if speaking of a convenience store. In other cities, cremation grounds are traditionally placed outside the city gates, to the south. Here, they burn at the center of all life.

I went back to my hotel to take this all in. "Everything is in flux," my young Virgil had told me as we walked along the river. "Everything is a constant succession of becomings. Nothing remains the same."

Next morning, a little before dawn, I walked out of the gates of the rickety palace to go down to the river again. Only one man was standing there, under a tree, holding his bicycle-rickshaw, his eyes angry and ablaze, and what looked to be a bullet hole in his cheek. We negotiated for a while, he agreed to take me to the holy waters, to wait there for two hours and to bring me back for under three dollars, and we took off into the gloom, the previously crowded streets under a kind of sorcerer's spell, quite empty.

To travel by bicycle in the dawn is to draw close to all the sounds, the smells, the ancient ghosts of Varanasi; for more than a week, the bicycle-rickshaw man would become my faithful friend, waiting outside the gates of the hotel, ready to guide me anywhere in the predawn hours or after dark. The winter fog compounded the half-dreamed air of the place, as figures loomed out of the mist to stare at us and then, as abruptly, vanished, as if nothing was quite substantial here, or even true. "Unreal City"—I found myself recalling my boyhood ingestion of T. S. Eliot, himself recalling Dante. "Under the brown fog of a winter dawn . . . I had not thought death had undone so many."

On the Ganges, a Charon pulled me soundlessly across the water, past all the broken palaces, the huge flights of steps, the men and women walking down to the water, barely clothed, dipping their heads in and shaking themselves dry, as if awakening from a long sleep. "In Varanasi," said the ferryman, as one of his colleagues led a fog-swaddled boat off to the other shore, "thirty-five, forty percent is holy men." Along the shore, a man was walking among visitors, muttering, "Memory card, memory card." In another boat, an Indian man here with his young wife and child had his laptop open in the phantasmal dark. Figures in blankets appeared through the mist, and cows, pariah dogs, red-bottomed monkeys trotted in and out of the temples. "Sir," said the boatman, and I braced myself for an offer of young girls, young boys or drugs, forgetting that the main thing on offer here was transformation. "You would like darshan? I arrange meeting with holy man for you?"

All this, I knew, was the Varanasi of sightseers, the Boschian riddle at the eye of the storm that entices many, horrifies others and leaves most of us feeling we're losing our minds, and don't know quite what to replace them with. But part of the power of the holy city is that it is shaped very consciously—like a mandala, some say, a series of concentric sacred zones—and as I moved away from the river, I came out into a world that is India's highest center of learning and scholarship, what Sir Edwin Arnold, the Victorian poet who rendered into English blank verse the life of the Buddha, had called "the Oxford and Canterbury of India in one."

"It really is such a beautiful city," said Pramod Chandra, an elegant soul who comes from a long line of Varanasi scholars and writers (and who had been, until recently, a professor of art at Harvard). We were seated in his large, bare family house not far from the flames of the burning ghats and crumbling palaces, and I was meeting him for the first time, on the advice of an American friend. "If they did it up, it could be another Sevilla, like one of the great cities of Spain or Italy. The tall houses in the Old City? If you go inside, you find abundant worlds there—courtyards and inner spaces, everything."

I thought, as he spoke, of the city where Varanasi saris

are spun into life by old men seated on the rooftops, working gold thread into white silk, and the city where musicians play on those same rooftops on hot summer nights (most of India's great classical musicians come from Varanasi). The previous day, at the Bharat Kala Bhavan Museum, set among mango trees and cricket pitches on the expansive, gracious campus of Banaras Hindu University, I had seen exquisite Buddhas shining through the often lightless spaces, as in some dusty Oxford attic, while nursing students in navy blue pullovers and white saris hurried towards their anatomy classes. "People always think of Benares as a place of pilgrimage," Professor Chandra went on, using the classical name for his city, "and they forget that it has always been an important trading place. This is where things go often to the west, all the way to Bombay. Silk, lacquer, textiles, indigo: they're all coming from here."

Its other, less tangible treasures now headed even farther west: the idea of reincarnation, the dissolution of distinctions between sacred and profane. Unlike in Jerusalem or Ladakh, it's not stones or monuments that give the city its sense of continuity; the buildings here were said to be only 350 years old. It was ideas and the customs passed down from one generation to the next that made the centuries blur.

"It could really be so beautiful," the old professor went on, smiling, "if only they did something with the palaces.

When I was a boy, jewelers came to the house and simply emptied the contents of their bags on the table. Diamonds, rubies, every kind of precious gem: you just took what you wanted and they didn't even bother to count it. They came back another day to collect the payment."

As he thought back to those days, his mind, perhaps inevitably, returned to the less visible gems he'd collected, at a time when learned men came to the big houses to teach Sanskrit, and fortunate boys committed long passages of holy text to memory.

"I can still remember the first two books of *Paradise Lost*," the seventy-eight-year-old professor announced, a gleam in his eye, and, without a pause, he began to declaim the whole story leading up to the Fall of Man.

The past itself might have been his Garden, I thought. Nothing can live up to the scenes that memory softens and gilds—even in a place where, in Octavio Paz's words, "Yesterday is today; the past returns; the future has already happened." But then I thought of the end of the poem the professor was reciting, and what was for me perhaps its most beautiful line: Adam's task, the archangel who accompanies him to the gates of Eden observes, is to find "a Paradise within thee, happier far."

It was, of course, the Buddha's message, too, the reason he had left his palace and delivered his first discourse, six miles from where we were sitting, on the fact of suffering and the ways we have to work through it. Paradise has to be found not just in the middle of life, but in the midst of death; this city of burning bodies was a little like the skull on a monastic's desk, reminding us that time is never so limitless as we think.

Before our evening ended, however, Professor Chandra had a deeper and even more intimate secret to impart. "Did your father ever tell you we were classmates?"

"At university in England?"

"No, no," he said. "At Antonio da Silva," the less-than-famous school in the dusty suburbs of Bombay that had not seemed the most obvious place to be sending students off to Harvard and Oxford.

He spun out stories of my grandmother, of my father as a teenager, whole pieces of my past that I could never have learned elsewhere; in opening up his past, he was throwing open the windows to my own.

The comfort of Varanasi, I'd imagined, before I arrived, was that I was unaffiliated here; I'd sought out the holy places of the Ethiopians, the Tibetans, the Muslims and the Jews before I ever dared to set foot in the place that was notionally mine. "Don't go to Varanasi," my relatives across India had often warned me. "It's just stench and crooks and dirt." Neither of my parents, lifelong students of religion born to Hinduism's priestly caste, had ever come here.

But now, as I stepped out of the stately house and towards my bicycle-rickshaw in the dark, I saw that it wasn't so far from me at all, the places we avoid so often closer to us than the ones we eagerly seek out.

———

Next day, I knew I had to make the trip out to Sarnath, where the Buddha, having walked away from the ritualism and abstraction of Brahman priests, had tried to explain the ways in which we could be physicians to ourselves. I'd been told that the appropriate way to make the twenty-minute trip was by pony cart, but I didn't want to leave my loyal bicycle-rickshaw driver behind. So I asked him if he was up for it, and, without a murmur, he nodded yes.

As we rode out into open fields and narrow roads, we might have been reenacting the young prince's own journey away from the city. The roar and frenzy of the streets began to fade, and we started to see temples, signs for the "Society for Human Perception," monks in gray or yellow robes glancingly visible between the trees. At the central park, once filled with deer, where the Buddha had delivered his first discourse, pilgrims gathered in silence in front of a stupa originally set up here 249 years before the birth of Christ.

Because the Dalai Lama happened to be offering teachings here during this week of thick fog, the space around the Dhamekh Stupa had turned into a busy, merry Tibetan settlement. Monks in bright red robes were seated in lines of three or four across the grass, reading from sutras or chanting. Twenty or so well-dressed foreigners were sitting in the lotus position, eyes tightly closed. Four Tibetan women whose ragged clothes suggested they had walked here across high passes were standing in a line and, one after another, raising joined palms before them, then flinging themselves down on the ground in a full three-part prostration before the temple.

No crackling flames here or men in ash; just mountain devotion as worn-faced grandmothers with gray pigtails walked around and around the stupa, telling their beads, and men from eastern Tibet with red pieces of string in their hair exchanged stories of their journey here, while young Tibetans in sunglasses joined their elders in circumambulation. I did, too—people around me were flinging ceremonial white scarves up towards ledges twenty or thirty feet above—and soon I could imagine that I was turning the wheel of time myself, playing out some eternal cycle of existence as I walked round and round, each circling bringing me a new set of neighbors.

I thought then of the stirring words of the Franciscan priest Richard Rohr: our goal in life, he often stressed, is not to become spiritual, but to become human. That was, of course, the heart of the Buddha's teaching as well, and the sense of potential he passed on to anyone who cared to listen: each of us has the capacity, through the discerning use of our minds, to see past some of our ignorance and come to terms with life as it is.

Around me—the Dalai Lama had concluded his talk for the day, on why the enlightened come back to the world to serve others—the little lanes were filling with so many maroon-robed monks, spilling out to chat or drink tea to-gether, as a full moon rose above the village walls, that I might have been in Lhasa again, risen from its ashes.

I recalled how the Zen teacher Eido-roshi, thinking of the cries of abandonment of Jesus upon the cross, had delivered a teaching that must have unsettled many of his students. "The struggle of your life," he'd said, "is your paradise."

———

That evening, back in the city, a huge moon now high above the water, I mounted the winding steps in a little guesthouse, tucked into a narrow street along the river, up to its roof, where vegetarian dinners were being served at a communal table. I fell into conversation there with the woman beside me, and learned that she was from Denmark, a psychiatrist, and had been living for ten months in Iraq, in the middle of the war.

Varanasi pulls such souls, I thought—she had no official reason for being here—and as she described her work in Sri Lanka and Rwanda, working for four years in the Balkans after the genocide, I caught a glimpse of why she had made her way to this dusty maelstrom. Her job, she said, was working with the consequences of conflict; she traveled to war zones to help people talk their way through their sufferings, so as to put the past—perhaps a devouring future, too—behind them.

"And Varanasi?"

"I think it's a pilgrimage of sorts," she said. "The whole of life, actually: trying to make sense of oneself, trying to come to terms with early traumas."

We picked at our vegetables, as a soft ring of chants rose up from the muddy alleyway far below.

"My mother left when I was four," she said. "My father took me to England and gave me to a family and then he left, too."

"Forever?"

"For eight months. Which, when you are four, feels forever."

She shook her shoulder-length red hair, as if to dispel the thought. Bangles jangled around her wrist.

"So all your work in war zones perhaps has something to do with this?"

"Oh, definitely," she said and then, as if to conclude the conversation, "they're all part of the same puzzle."

Then we headed downstairs to the living room, where a sitarist and a tabla player were taking their seats on a carpet on the floor. A small figure with tufts of white hair around his bald head came in and sat down in front of me. He turned round to see who was there and, when he caught sight of me, offered a casual nod; I'd met Peter, I realized, three years earlier, in the Tiergarten in Berlin, where he, a German singer of Sufi ghazals, had spun me enchanting tales of Ethiopia and Mali.

———

I'd been speaking to the Dalai Lama for more than thirty years when I arrived in Varanasi, and one thing that always moved me was that he was constantly in the thick of things, on the streets of India, where so many are in crying need, visiting Belfast and Jerusalem, going to the places where life and death seem overpowering. It was relatively easy to find paradise, I'd found, on top of a mountain, or in my Benedictine monastery; but he, like his friend Archbishop Tutu or Mother Teresa, like the young Dutch woman Etty Hillesum, was never set away from us, never distant from our sorrow or confusion. Sometimes, in fact, I wondered if anyone I knew had suffered more: nine of the sixteen children his mother would bear died young, the government of the largest nation on earth called him a demon and he'd had to try to protect six million people from across a distant border for half a century.

Yet no one I knew was better able to project confidence, or readier to smile and laugh. In all our time together, I always saw him avoid the otherworldly; the meaning of life, he said, lies in what we can do right now. When people came to him in search of blessings, he stressed that he was no miracle worker. "You bless yourself with your actions," he explained. "For example, give money to a school." Once, in a private audience, I'd seen a Korean man exclaim, in his excitement, "You will go to the Pure Land!" The Dalai Lama replied by quoting the First Dalai Lama: "I don't want to go to the Pure Land. I want to serve where I am needed."

So as I came back from Sarnath, I decided that I would no longer seek out holy places in this city of temples; I would just let life come to me in all its happy confusion and find the holiness in that. I sat where I was, along the river, and watched the carnival play out.

A crow was sitting on a placid cow, now and then pecking bits of seed off the cow's cheek. A sage of some kind fielded a cricket ball from the river and flung it back to the boys who had set up a high-speed game along the banks.

Gypsies from the backpack trail drifted past, swathed in scarves and shawls, as Indian boys ran beside them, pestering them with questions. Another boat took an overload of pilgrims off to the sand-colored, distant shore.

A compendium of all the world's pleasures and confusions, the churning current of Varanasi threw everything and its opposite together, and declared all of it holy. It reminded me of what Thomas Merton had found in the smiling Buddhas of Sri Lanka, "filled with every possibility, questioning nothing, knowing everything, rejecting nothing." It explained why the extreme renunciates here lived beside graves and drank from skulls, having ceased to make any distinction between purity and its opposite. As Merton had put it, with unflinching economy, "The more you try to avoid suffering, the more you suffer."

Walking back towards where the flames were devouring some stranger, I started to imagine, as never before, what it would be like to see my sweetheart's body crumbling and cracking before my eyes, the shoulder I had grown used to holding, every day for twenty years, the bright eyes that had always held me captive, gone. I saw her as ash, or sitting beside my ashes.

A little girl with a bucket walked calmly among the burning corpses, as a dog nearby, ribs sticking out from its haunches, foraged for spare flesh. Above us, a cow was watching from a temple terrace, while the man beside me stood next to a small worn pan, selling nuts as at a base-ball game. Just behind the fire-lit hallucination, a "Night Cafe" was advertising "A.C. Restaurent, with Gift Shop (Ispecially for Indian Food)."

I started to walk then, all the way along the river to the south, till I came to another burning ghat, orange flames lighting up the surrounding buildings. As I continued, the path grew darker and more deserted, till the only light came from far above, where a small candle was flickering inside a rounded shrine. I walked on, away from the light, know-ing the walkways of the city so well by now that I could dodge the areas where the water buffalo relieved them-selves, avoid the kite strings of little boys who raced along the riverbank as if to tangle us all up in Varanasi itself.

I couldn't see it in the dark, but I was aware, as always, of the low, bare sandbank on the other shore, towards which ferrymen were bearing their passengers. In the distance, a dull orange light gleamed. The decaying palaces, with their hollowed-out windows and their interiors stuffed with re-fuse or with huddled bodies, looked, when a light came on, like the homes of celebrants at some great festival who had long passed on, ghost houses. A red-bottomed monkey was wailing piteously, and a goat of many colors was ambling past. Somewhere behind me, in the Vishwanath Temple, newcomers were handing over pens to a nearby shopkeeper, since even instruments of writing are, in the holy city, taken to be potential weapons.

A crossing-ground, I began to think, is not just a place where the dead move on to something else, but where the living can step across a boundary, too, into a different way of apprehending everything. "For Hindus," I had read in the work of the Varanasi scholar Diana Eck, "death is not the opposite of life; it is, rather, the opposite of birth," akin, perhaps, to leaving a cinema by a different exit from the one you came in by. A journey beginning in bright summer sunlight could usefully end in clouds.

The next morning I ran into my guide from the first day, always eager to show visitors the beauties of "my city."

"How are you, my friend?" I called.

"So good, sir. It is a beautiful day. More warm. No fog. Visibility is good."

"So you think the curse is lifted?"

"Oh, yes, sir. This all means it is the coming of spring."

One morning later, my last in Varanasi, I woke to find the whole city covered in a thick pall of mist, so thick that the ghostly towers and palaces I had seen from my room seemed to have unmade themselves in the dark. Planes would be unable to take off or land. Trains would be delayed twenty hours or more. Vehicles would crash into one another, with fatal results. Down by the river, on my farewell visit, I could not see thirty feet in front of me. Smoke from all the fires, mixed with winter fog and pollution, made every figure look even more like a visitor from another world. It was easy to believe we were all caught up in the same spell, creatures in some celestial dream, ferried silently across the river and back again, part of a cycle from which we could never be detached. It was easy, in fact, to imagine that we were all caught up now in this half known realm, and a candlelit back alleyway would be the only true home—the deepest paradise—we could ever hope to find.

Acknowledgements

Two friends deserve most of the credit for this book: my wonderfully spirited, tireless and fun comrade-in-arms since 1993, Lynn Nesbit, who sprang into action even during a global lockdown to make sure my words would find a happy and sustaining home; and my editor, Jynne Dilling Martin, who threw her brilliant mind and unparalleled energy into this work as if it were one of her own books of poetry (from Antarctica, perhaps).

I can't remember meeting anyone who, after a quick first reading of a very rough draft, would send along a thirteen-page, single-spaced, beautifully kind and detailed letter, alight with references to the Marathon Monks of Mount Hiei, haunting Sufi fables, even memories of her many trips to Ladakh, as well as a perfect quote from Wallace Stevens. I'll never know what I did right to get such an electric, original, warmhearted and discerning friend by my side, but I profited immensely from Jynne's every last searching perception and delicate glint of poetry.

At Riverhead, I also owe warm thanks to Geoff Kloske, Helen Yentus, Ashley Sutton, Ashley Garland, Katie Hurley, Sheila Moody, Will Jeffries, Mike Brown, Bianca Flores, Nora Alice Demick and Stephanie Hwang; and at Janklow & Nesbit, to Mina Hamedi and Michael Steger, among many others. I'm forever grateful to the incomparably attentive Miriam Feuerle and her all-star team at the Lyceum Agency. And at my old professional home, I never got a chance to thank properly such constantly patient and generous colleagues as Sarah Nisbet, Rita Madrigal, Tom Pold and Vanessa Haughton, who've supported me in so many ways, season after season, tending to my every last need with extraordinary kindness and enthusiasm and grace.

In my private life, I can never offer sufficient thanks to four selfless friends of nearly half a century: Russ and Gerry Lewin and Carl and Christine Nolt. To Roman Baratiak and Celesta Bilecci, who've kept me going somehow, in all kinds of ways, through thick and thin. To my long-suffering editors abroad, Michael Fishwick and Meru Gokhale.

The irreplaceable Robert Silvers, cofounder and editor, for fifty-four years, of *The New York Review of Books*, committed the rash act of taking writers to be priceless assets—invaluable caretakers of our conscience—and assuming that rigorous reports of our global neighborhood were essential to our survival. During the twenty-two years I was so delightedly writing for him, I was also very grateful to Klara Glowczewska and Hanya Yanagihara, to Graydon Carter and Katherine Stirling, to Nathan Lump, Rahul Jacob and Adi Ignatius, for sending me out to some of the places I describe in this book and for understanding how urgent it is to observe other cultures firsthand and then share those observations with the world.

A Note on the Author

Pico Iyer was born in Oxford to parents from India, raised in California and educated in England and the US. Since 1987, he has been based in western Japan, while travelling everywhere from Antarctica to Easter Island. He is the acclaimed author of sixteen books which have been translated into twenty-three languages. His last book, *A Beginner's Guide to Japan*, was the winner of the Edward Stanford APA Publications Travel Memoir of the Year 2020. His journalism appears regularly in the *Financial Times*, the *New York Times* and many other places, and his four TED talks have been viewed more than eleven million times.